The Clever SELF CARE GUIDE

DR NADINE HAMILTON

Other books by Nadine Hamilton
Coping With Stress and Burnout as a Veterinarian

First published 2023 by:
Australian Academic Press Group Pty. Ltd.
Samford Valley, Australia
www.australianacademicpress.com.au

Copyright © 2023 Nadine Hamilton

Copying for educational purposes
The *Australian Copyright Act 1968* (Cwlth) allows a maximum of one chapter or 10% of this book, whichever is the greater, to be reproduced and/or communicated by any educational institution for its educational purposes provided that the educational institution (or the body that administers it) has given a remuneration notice to Copyright Agency Limited (CAL) under the Act.

For details of the CAL licence for educational institutions contact:
Copyright Agency Limited, 19/157 Liverpool Street, Sydney, NSW 2000.
E-mail info@copyright.com.au

Production and communication for other purposes
Except as permitted under the Act, for example a fair dealing for the purposes of study, research, criticism or review, no part of this book may be reproduced, stored in a retrieval system, or transmitted in any form or by any means electronic, mechanical, photocopying, recording or otherwise without prior written permission of the copyright holder.

 A catalogue record for this book is available from the National Library of Australia

ISBN 9781925644579 (paperback)
ISBN 9781925644586 (ebook)

DISCLAIMER: Every effort has been made in preparing this work to provide information based on accepted evidence, standards and practice at the time of publication. By referring to this book, any and all readers release the author and publisher of any claims of direct or consequential damages resulting from relying on the content contained herein.

Publisher & Editor: Stephen May
Cover design: Luke Harris, Working Type Studio
Typesetting: Australian Academic Press
Printing: Lightning Source

This book is dedicated to my amazing husband Kirk, who I met and started dating in 1988 and married over three decades ago in 1992.

Kirk you are my absolute rock, biggest supporter, sounding board, and personal cheer squad — I wouldn't be the person I am without you.

I love you.

Foreword

Life is hard. Period. The Buddhists say the sooner we accept this, the easier life becomes. Many of us are waiting for life to get easier before we find the time to care for ourselves. Unfortunately, this rarely happens. Too often I see in clinical practice those of us who have neglected our physical and mental health for so long that we have reached the point of burnout. Yet, this can be avoided if we learn to make the time along the way to invest in a little self-care. I've learnt this the hard way a few too many times (I'm a slow learner).

Like many of us professionals, being a hard-working, high-achieving perfectionist who puts everyone else's needs before my own (and being a parent just adds to this), I have let my health come second to the point of absolute exhaustion. The old saying of do as I say and not as I do can hold true for many of us. But I'm working on it! I realise that the older we get and the more we have taken advantage of our bodies, the less likely we are to bounce back from burnout. But self-care is vital if we are to continue being of sound health and mind to be of continued service to others.

As I mentioned in my first book, *Healthy Habits: 52 Ways to Better Health*, which I wrote as much for myself and for my patients, making time to nurture ourselves can often feel selfish, but self-care is so critical to mental and physical health that I would argue we need to place it at the top of our priority list. This is not only important when we feel worn out physically or mentally but also to prevent us from going further south with our health. It is so easy to just keep going without taking stock of how we are feeling about our lives, our health and our current relationships. But sooner or later, unless we start really nurturing ourselves, we find that we begin to resent our families, our friends, our work and our once enjoyable commitments for taking up all our time. The unfortunate result of this is frustration, fatigue, self-loathing, and lack of overall enjoyment in our lives. The remedy to feeling this way is to realise we are the masters of our bodies, our actions, our thoughts, and our schedules and to make a little time to self-nurture.

I must admit, I'm a glass-half-empty kind of person. Call it being realistic, seeing things only in black or white, or just plain pessimism; I simply can't help it. Or so I thought! What I now realise is that thinking optimistically is a habit. Some of us just need to work a little harder at forming this mental habit. But if we are to cope with life's challenges, and let's face it, life is full of those, then we need to have a perspective that is more rose-coloured than not. In my 15 years of clinical practice, I can certainly attest that those that err on the side of seeing the good in every situation tend to be able to move through it and past it rather than getting emotionally stuck. Much of self-care has to do with our psychology.

That's where *The Clever Self-Care Guide* comes in. This well-thought-out and easy-to-follow guide on understanding self-care and how to incorporate it into our lives is a must in my opinion for all busy professionals. Through Nadine's extensive experience as a psychologist, she has spoken right to the heart of the issues blocking our ability to truly self-care. Learning to self-care is a skill, and for some of us, it is a lifelong learning process, but the sooner we learn it, the sooner we can get on with living to our fullest potential without burnout and its debilitating fatigue!

Dr. Cris Beer FRACGP, FASLM, FACNEM, MBBS(hons), BBiomedSci
Author of *Healthy Habits: 52 Ways to Better Health, Healthy Liver* and *Your Best Year Ahead: Small, Easy Steps to Wellness.*

Acknowledgments

Firstly, thank you to Stephen May, my publisher, for taking the chance on me with my first book *Coping with Stress and Burnout as a Veterinarian* which went on to become a bestseller. I dearly hope this book will be bigger and better than the last! Thank you for this wonderful opportunity to publish my second book.

Thank you to the many friends, family, colleagues, acquaintances, and clients throughout my life who have reminded me — often inadvertently — of the importance of looking after ourselves.

My colleague and friend Janine McEvoy — thank you for being my 'debrief buddy' when I need advice or support — personally and professionally. I love how we can chat openly for hours (and hours) and it seems like no time has passed. Thank you for encouraging me to become an EMDR practitioner — it is one of the best things I could have done!

To my fellow authors whose self-help books and work inspire me daily — thank you. I do not profess to know everything there is to know about self-care and am grateful to have other professionals sharing their wisdom with me.

My amazing doctor, Dr Cris Beer, thank you for listening to me and my health challenges, and not dismissing me like many other doctors had. I am forever grateful to have you as my healthcare practitioner, guiding me on my own journey to excellent health, wellbeing, and self-care. I am honoured to have you write the Foreword of this book — thank you!

Dori Martin, FDN-P — not only an incredible health practitioner who has helped me immensely with my health journey over the years, but my special 'twinsie'. I truly value and appreciate you and am so blessed to have you as a friend and business partner.

Saving the best until last — my beautiful family! Kirk, Cheyenne, and Jaimie (and of course our umpteen pets!) you are my world. Thank you for giving me the space and support to do the work I love (and then write books about it!), and practice my own self-care. I love you all to the moon and back (and then some!).

About the Author

Dr Nadine Hamilton has worked as a psychologist for nearly two decades. She is recognised as a global leader in veterinary wellbeing through her ground-breaking research and years of professional work with veterinary practice managers and owners to increase wellbeing, productivity, and retention in the workplace. In support of her aim to create a paradigm shift within the veterinary industry, in 2018, she founded the charity *Love Your Pet Love Your Vet*, which raises awareness about mental health issues within the veterinary industry. She published her first book in 2019 — *Coping With Stress and Burnout as a Veterinarian* — an evidence-based resource to help vets build protective attitudes, enhanced wellbeing, and increased coping skills to try and prevent the psychological distress that can lead to self-harm.

Nadine's journey to 'now' wasn't always easy. She failed her high school exams and dropped out at just 15 years of age, but this did not deter her from following her dreams. She has worked in many different industries in various roles, such as clerk, dental nurse, office manager, personal assistant, teacher/trainer, rehabilitation consultant, lecturer, and acting head of department. As well as being a registered psychologist, she holds a Master of

Training and Development degree, a Doctor of Education, and qualifications in nutritional psychiatry, Feng Shui, and healing.

She set up her psychology clinic, *Positive Psych Solutions*, in 2010. The clinic provides a wide range of online courses, eBooks, live workshops and wellbeing plans and programs. You can read more about the services offered by Dr Nadine and her team at Positive Psych Solutions by visiting www.positivepsychsolutions.com.au.

Contents

Foreword v

Acknowledgments ix

About the Author xi

Introduction 1

Chapter 1 What is Self-care? 3

Chapter 2 Healthy Self-esteem 17

Chapter 3 Mindfulness 25

Chapter 4 Changing Careers 29

Chapter 5 Setting Boundaries 37

Chapter 6 Stress 51

Chapter 7 Dealing with Anxiety 63

Chapter 8 Dealing with Depression 71

Chapter 9 Coping with Grief 77

Chapter 10 Coping with Change and Adversity 83

Chapter 11 Compassion Fatigue 91

Chapter 12 Burnout 97

Chapter 13 Dealing with Imposter Syndrome 105

Chapter 14 Coping Strategies 111

Chapter 15 Relaxation 131

Chapter 16 Resilience 137

Chapter 17 Spirituality 141

Chapter 18 Motivation 145

Chapter 19 Exploring Core Beliefs 149

Chapter 20 Mental Health Problems
 need Mental Health Solutions 155

Chapter 21 Mentally Healthy Workplaces 163

Chapter 22 The Importance of Hope and Optimism 171

Here's to your Wellbeing 177

Bibliography 179

Introduction

'A smooth sea never made a skilled sailor'
— Franklin D. Roosevelt.

It's hard to believe it's been four years since my first book, *Coping with Stress and Burnout as a Veterinarian*, was published in 2019. Written in response to high levels of mental distress within the veterinary community that place vet staff at significant risk for suicide, the book provided an examination of the unique aspects of veterinary work that contributed to the problem as well as psychological principles and tools to help improve it. The book was based on my own Doctoral research as well as years of consulting and therapy work with vet staff. It has been used worldwide in thousands of vet practices, and I have received tremendous feedback on its ability to help so many people in their daily life. In examining this gratifying success and continuing to work with a range of clients both in and out of the veterinary profession, I realised that there was a clear need for more practical wellbeing tips for not just vet staff, but everyone dealing with difficulties in life. We can all do with the best quality of mental health and resilience to deal with today's complicated and scary world.

So much has happened since 2019 to add to the challenges of work-life, family life, and social life that now more than ever, we need effective psychological tools for better mental wellbeing that are able to be easily learned by clear, concise advice. After adjusting to my own professional and personal changes over the past few years, I have found myself talking with clients (and myself) more and more about the importance of looking after yourself. Self-care is a vital skill to learn and apply in our lives because life is always full of things that can rock our boat so strongly we are at risk of drowning. Yet, as exemplified in the wonderful quote above from Franklin D. Roosevelt, learning to adapt to different situations makes us better at coping with the tosses and turns of life.

In this book, I will talk about the importance of self-care and how we can use knowledge and tools to help us navigate life's ups and downs. We will cover topics such as setting boundaries, dealing with stress and anxiety, mentally healthy workplaces, and the imperative to build more hope and optimism into our daily lives.

My hope is that you will find this book helpful and informative, but also that you will be able to adopt and adapt some of the strategies I cover and apply them to your daily life – so you too can love the life you live.

Let's get started!

Chapter 1

What is Self-care?

Self-care might seem like a fluffy word or the latest 'buzz' word going around, but it truly is important. But what does it mean?

Some people may view self-care as mainly about physical behaviours such as exercising, doing yoga, eating nutritiously, and so on. But it is so much more than this. Self-care also includes looking after our psychological and spiritual health, just as much as our physical health. The concept of mind–body–spirit automatically comes to mind for me when I think of self-care, and I'm a firm believer that we need to take a holistic approach to our wellbeing if we want to nurture and nourish ourselves for optimal wellbeing. Self-care therefore involves attending to a range of important aspects in our lives. Here's a quick rundown before we dive deeper in this book about the 'how' of dealing with these issues.

Dealing with stress

Stress. When I think back to a job I worked in over 20 years ago, I can recall one of my colleagues confiding in me that she felt stressed — but her doctor had told her not to tell the bosses because they may perceive it as a sign of weakness! Instead, the doctor wrote on her medical certificate that she was suffering from a 'medical condition'. Back then, we didn't really talk about stress — there seemed to be such a big taboo around it, but these days it's as if it's almost compulsory! How often do we talk about being stressed or feeling stressed out? It seems so commonplace today that it's hard to believe it was such a sensitive topic in what seems like just a few years ago.

As I will discuss in an upcoming chapter, there are different types of stress. There is the 'good' stress called eustress, and the not-so-good stress called distress. The aim is to balance the two, ideally with less distress. Eustress can be the type of stress that motivates us — like getting all our things packed for a long-awaited holiday or picking that perfect outfit for a hot date. Once the situation is over, the stress dissipates. Whereas with distress, it tends to linger and/or cause negative symptoms — this is the kind of stress we may feel if we are experiencing financial problems, work conflict, relationship issues, and so on. The kind that makes us feel sick to our stomach, keeps us awake at night, and affects our ability to think and act clearly. We definitely don't want this type of stress lingering!

But even though it feels like we have been programmed to believe that all stress is 'bad', there are actually some simple things you can do to try and identify stress early and take a proactive approach to manage it in a healthier way. In addition to the tips I'll share with you in the chapter on stress, here are a couple of actions to consider:

- Take a mindful moment each day to reflect and enjoy immersing yourself in journalling (or even just

keeping a list of) all the things you have accomplished over the past few days.
- Be mindful of your body language. It has been said that our mind can change our bodies, and our bodies can change our minds. When you display and adopt positive body language, it can help you to become more resilient, optimistic, and perseverant — and it increases testosterone by up to 20% and decreases cortisol! Together, high testosterone and low cortisol have been shown to help people make decisions, deal with deadlines, and thrive under pressure. It helps you have a clear and confident mind, boosts your emotional intelligence, and changes your spirit by making you more likeable and conveying competence.

Food, mood, and hormones

There is a lot of research coming out at present about the gut-brain axis and its connection to food and mood — particularly with depression. Originally it was thought that depression was purely a result of a chemical imbalance in the brain. However, emerging research now suggests it may not be — rather, that it is due to issues with the gut-brain axis.

There is also a lot of research and evidence connecting the food we eat with the effects on our mood — even to the level of food intolerances being connected to anxiety, stress, depression, and even suicide! I personally think it's quite refreshing to know that it may not all be 'in our head' as once believed. Rather it could be 'in our gut' (aka 'the second brain') instead. And once we understand this connection and feed our body healthy and nutritious foods, it is amazing how much better we can feel!

Two of my good friends and colleagues are qualified nutritionists and they often speak about 'food being medicine'. I think this is so important to know first-hand the impact food can have on the body. There are many people like me who suffer from food intolerances or allergies (intolerances and allergies are not the same) and those who have more serious conditions. The connection between what goes in our mouths and how we feel is strong.

One thing I noticed a few years ago was my level of hunger when I was feeling stressed and had a lousy night's sleep. I wondered if there was a connection between feeling tired and feeling hungry. Then I found out about two very important hormones — ghrelin and leptin.

Ghrelin is the hormone that stimulates hunger (i.e., signals that you are hungry), and leptin is the hormone that suppresses or inhibits hunger (i.e. signals you are full). Some interesting things happen when these two get involved — particularly with sleep and weight loss. When you don't get the appropriate level and quality of sleep, these two hormones basically start to misbehave. Ghrelin goes into overdrive, and leptin goes to sleep on the job — meaning, you may feel hungrier than normal, despite having just eaten!

When we talk about these two hormones in terms of weight loss, there are some strange things that happen. As you lose weight:

- You get hungrier as ghrelin increases.

- Then GLP-1 (glucagon-like peptide-1) decreases — so you get even hungrier.
- Your hunger isn't as suppressed because leptin decreases as the fat cells in your body become smaller.
- You feel less satiated because CCK (cholecystokinin) and PYY (gastric-inhibitory polypeptide YY) decrease.
- Cortisol (aka the 'stress' hormone) increases — and high stress equals high cortisol levels, which equals problems processing what you eat.

Nutritional Psychiatry
While still on the topic of nutrition, nutritional psychiatry is an emerging field that essentially looks at how food and nutrients can treat and prevent mental illness. There is a lot of evidence to support nutritional psychiatry and how important the food/mood and gut-brain axis really is for our overall health and wellbeing. Nutritional deficiencies have been linked to mental illness, and three neuro-nutrients in particular have been identified to help with your brain's experience and processing of emotions. These are serotonin, fermented foods, and vitamin D (yes — vitamin D! Did you know it's been used in the prevention and treatment of depression, anxiety, and some other mental illnesses?).

As mentioned, food relates to addictions, anxiety, psychotic disorders, and depression. The gut-brain connection (aka the gut-brain axis) is essential as the gut bacteria (microbiome) sends chemical signals to your brain. When your microbiome is healthy, the messages sent to the brain are more reliable and trustworthy, whereas when your microbiome is not good, the messages being sent are not going to be as helpful.

We need a healthy gut for a healthy brain — mental health is brain health.

Exercise

High-intensity activity (i.e., bursts of very intense cardio activities) has been reported to immediately suppress hunger — and for up to 48 hours afterwards. This positive effect is believed to be due to the activity decreasing ghrelin and increasing leptin sensitivity. On the other hand, aerobic activity performed at a low/moderate level (such as a swim or brisk walking) has been shown to increase ghrelin and decrease leptin — that is, it may make you feel hungry. I am sure many of us can relate to this result, and why it can explain my hunger levels increasing after lower-intensity exercise! Still, both exercise approaches are beneficial.

From a self-care perspective, exercise should be an integral component. It is well known that when we exercise, we release endorphins — those happy little chemicals that help us feel good. But did you know that you don't have to be doing high impact, high-intensity exercise to benefit? As with relaxation, I believe finding an exercise you enjoy should be important — so long as it is safe, healthy, and legal! However, being out in nature while exercising can be like a double whammy — you can benefit from moving your body while also enjoying the scenery! Have you ever felt like exercising doesn't seem like such hard work when you are doing something you enjoy? It's no secret that the beach is my happy place, and

I am incredibly lucky that I live on the coast and have access to some of the most beautiful beaches in the world. While I engage in other types of exercise, we try to get out to walk along the beach with our Labrador Jophiel at least two-or-three times per week. When we are walking along the sand, feeling the water run over our feet, and enjoying the scenery, it doesn't feel like exercise at all because it is such a pleasant experience.

You may enjoy hiking, surfing, cycling, or going for a run. Whatever it is, it is suggested you find something you enjoy so that you feel motivated to get out there and exercise. Alternatively, you might find exercises with qualified instructors through reputable apps or websites that you can do from home. I have used one such app for decades, allowing me to do my cardio exercises from the comfort and convenience of my air conditioned lounge room even in the height of a hot and humid Queensland summer. There's really no excuse to not exercise, so long as you are physically capable of doing so. (Best to get a check-up first from your local doctor if its been a while.)

If you are struggling to find an exercise program that works for you, it could be helpful to find a trained and qualified professional who can help you put a suitable program together. I personally worked with an exercise physiologist to help put a program together for me and who was able to adapt the training to accommodate my 'dodgy' knees.

Overexercising
There is no disputing then that exercise can be good for us — physically and psychologically, but too much can be harmful. Not only can overexercising lead to muscle

injury, joint injury, heart issues, and other physical injuries, it can also affect your brain and mental health by forming an addiction or even leading to low self-esteem and depression.

It is essential to think about your reasons for exercising — ask yourself, how will you feel if you don't do this workout (your response here could be a sign that your relationship with exercise might need some help). So, if you feel anxious or uneasy about not exercising, or you feel like you will have to compensate for it in another way, this could be a clue that you need to think about what your exercise relationship is really telling you.

Workplace Issues

As I will cover in a later chapter, workplace issues account for quite a lot of stress for many people, and workplace conflict is no exception. Given that some people spend such a large amount of their time at work, it is vital you look after yourself while at work.

While I will discuss boundaries and resilience a little later, if you are finding things stressful or overwhelming at work, there are a few quick-and-easy things you might like to try:

- Take a few minutes to do some deep breathing — even if you have to go into the bathroom and close the cubicle door. Deep breathing can help to slow your heart rate and try to bring your stress levels down.
- Talk with a trusted co-worker or friend. Social support is known to be a protective factor for good mental health, and speaking with someone you trust

can act as a distraction while at the same time it may help you to feel supported.

- Walk away for a few minutes to help you clear your mind — while you may need to do this in your break, if you feel like you aren't able to wait until your break, mention to your co-workers that you need to step outside for a few moments.

- Get the blood flowing by spending a few moments to stretch — ideally every hour if you can.

Resistance

While resistance may be helpful in the physical sense (such as resistance training), it can have both positive and not-so-positive effects in other aspects. Think of that resistant person who is determined not to let you in as you try to merge into traffic, or the child who refuses to get out of bed on a school morning, or perhaps a client you have who is adamant nothing you do will make a difference. On the flip side, resistance can also be used to help stop automatic behaviours — that is, you can resist buying into the temptation of those chocolate biscuits, or that extra drink, or sitting on the couch instead of going for a healthy walk.

When you are trying to use resistors for your self-care, think about unhelpful and perhaps unhealthy behaviours you engage in. Are these really benefiting your wellbeing? If not, and you are ready to try and break unhelpful behaviours, think of them as barriers or stop signs that make it harder to totally buy into that unhealthy habit.

There are three types of resistors:

- Mental resistors — these are the cognitive resistors

such as thoughts or self-talk that can help you to look at the long-term consequences or benefits of an action.

- Practical resistors — these are the practical things you can do to help slow down the automatic tendency to go from 0 to 100 in no time, such as deep breathing, going for a walk, or using different ways to cope with things.
- Physical resistors — these are more tangible such as objects or people who can get in your way, such as having that support person who physically steps in front of the fridge to stop you from reaching for that chocolate biscuit.

What kind of resistors do you need to help you change that unhealthy behaviour so you can start to put yourself — and your self-care — first? I'd suggest just picking one or two to begin with so that it's not so overwhelming and then focus on putting them into practice.

Positive Rewards

Sometimes we all feel like we need a treat, especially after a hard day, but it's important to recognise that they don't need to cost money or involve food and/or alcohol as many rewards tend to do.

There are different types of rewards we can use to help our self-care, such as:

- Healthy rewards — like taking a class at the gym, going for a walk, eating dinner at a healthy new restaurant, getting adequate sleep, buying a new healthy cookbook, riding a bike, or buying new workout clothes.

- Tangible rewards — such as books, new shoes, a new journal, or subscription to your favourite journal or podcast series.
- Social rewards — such as calling a friend, having a Zoom party, going for a picnic in the park, watching a comedy show, or going to the movies.
- Self-care rewards — such as taking a nap, colouring in, smelling flowers, reading a book, watching a movie, dancing, getting out in nature, or listening to music.

Even just being able to reward ourselves as part of our self-care routine can be helpful. Instead of spending hours of time on social media that you can't get back, why not invest that time in yourself and do something you really enjoy instead? During some recent time-off, I thoroughly enjoyed reading books and listening to music while I did some colouring-in. It was lovely to 'switch off' from the everyday demands I have and instead put that focus into something I found relaxing.

Try to pick one or two things you can do for your self-care each week, and make sure you implement them.

Goal Setting

While we talk about SMART goals (that is, goals that are Specific, Measurable, Achievable, Realistic, and Time-based), we can also think about performance and mastery-oriented goals.

Performance-oriented goals are those which focus on achieving some level of ability or competence at a specific task. For example, an athlete striving to improve their fitness or perfect a technique that will help them compete better. Or a person who is undertaking a course to learn new skills to perform their job better.

Mastery oriented goals are those which focus on developing new skills through learning, self-improvement, or mastering tasks. For example, learning how to play a musical instrument or fine-tuning your pilates or yoga exercises.

Having your goals oriented towards mastery is said to increase:

- performance
- engagement
- self-efficacy
- thirst for knowledge
- resilience when faced with failure.

Just like I mentioned above with finding some positive rewards you can implement each week, set some time aside to write out your SMART goals and then get set to start putting them into action. You could even start out by making your SMART goals around ways you will commit to self-care and looking after your wellbeing!

Resilience

On the topic of resilience, researchers from Yale University have reported that one of the greatest predictors of resilience is social support. Certainly, it is known that social support can be a protective factor for good mental health, so this research really comes as no surprise.

There is also evidence to suggest that the more oxytocin you have, the more resilience you have. If you haven't heard of oxytocin, it is a hormone that plays an integral part in sexual reproduction and social interaction (often called the 'cuddle' hormone). Your body produces oxytocin when you have positive interactions with others, which can help make you feel less stressed in the long run.

I will discuss resilience in more depth in Chapter 16, so I don't want to rehash it here. Suffice to say that resilience does not always come from trauma or adversity, but it can also be built from successes as well. So rather than being down on yourself for all your perceived failures, turn that frown upside down and focus on all your successes instead. They don't always have to be 'big' things either — sometimes just getting the lawns mowed, or the clothes ironed, or getting through a long shift at work could count as a success! And remember — success doesn't always mean money or financial success — being successful is so much more than being rich!

Boosting Endorphins

As you now know, when we exercise, it helps us to release endorphins — those happy little hormones secreted in the nervous system and brain that act as an antidepressant and pain reliever in the body. While you might like to think of this little boost of positivity as reinforcement for exercise, remember to consider your relationship with exercise. If you feel like you can't be happy without the endorphin boost from exercise, this may be a distorted thought.

The good news is that there are other ways to boost endorphins, such as:
- laughing
- stretching
- meditating

- enjoying a healthy snack
- smiling
- gifting or donating something
- love.

What are some of the positive ways you can think of to help boost your endorphins? So long as they are safe, healthy, and legal, why not add them to your SMART goal setting list and set out to engage in endorphin-boosting activities each day!

Chapter 2

Healthy Self-esteem

Let's look at some of the things that can contribute to how we feel about ourselves and our lives. There are many facets that can potentially 'make or break' our day, with one thing in particular underlying all these — our self-esteem.

Some of the factors that can have an impact include:
- attitudes and behaviours of others
- our mindset
- events during the day
- our coping mechanisms
- our resiliency
- our jobs and workplace
- our relationships
- our health
- our financial situation
- our personal circumstances.

How we feel and react to these factors can vary greatly. The better our self-esteem, the better we are likely to handle our feelings and reactions.

What is Self-esteem?

Self-esteem generally refers to a measure of worth about ourselves and/or aspects of ourselves, the value we place on ourselves as an individual, and how we think about and view ourselves. There can be both healthy self-esteem and low self-esteem. First, let's look at low self-esteem — what it is, the impacts, the beginnings of it, and what maintains it.

Low Self-esteem

Low self-esteem can develop when the value we put on ourselves is negative. Some examples include:

- thinking you are flawed
- feeling inferior to others
- thinking you're not good enough, you're weak, or you're stupid
- feeling unlovable, unattractive, and/or ugly
- thinking you're a failure or loser.

The kind of basic negative beliefs some people have about themselves and the type of person they are, are usually deep-seated and viewed (by themselves) as the truth or facts, rather than them seeing these are merely just their opinions about themselves.

Some impacts of low self-esteem are:

- a lack of personal self-care
- frequent self-criticism
- problems with relationships
- negative impacts on work or study
- ignoring one's positive qualities
- decreased leisure and recreational activities.

How does low self-esteem develop?

As shown in the diagram below, low self-esteem can develop from early life experiences that are perceived to be negative, which then lead to negative core beliefs, rules, and assumptions that are unhelpful. This then leads to unhelpful behaviour.

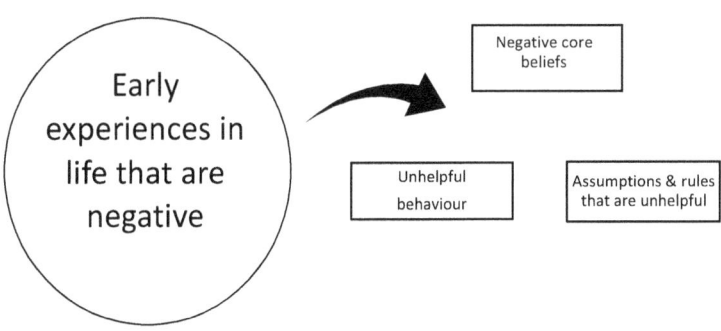

But I feel 'okay' most the time
While on the surface you could be feeling good about yourself — provided you live up to the standards and rules you have for yourself — there is the risk of experiencing dormant low self-esteem. At the slightest challenge or hiccup along the way, this low self-esteem could be woken at any time, especially due to the pressure on yourself to maintain and manage this self-esteem, and also because the negative core beliefs are reinforced as they are never tested or challenged.

How Self-esteem is maintained

The diagram below sets out how self-esteem is maintained.

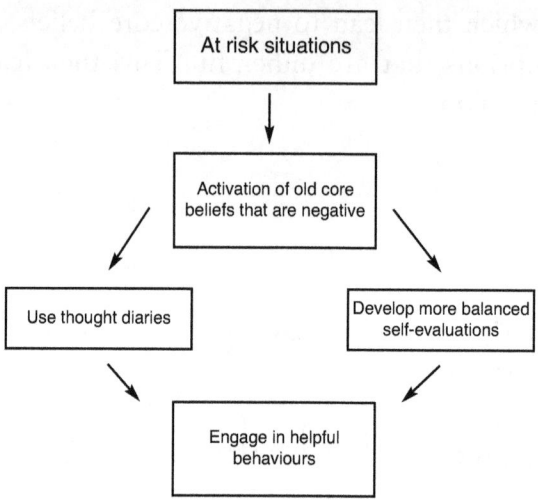

Addressing Self-esteem

Recognising and acknowledging your success and strengths, as well as what you perceive are your weaknesses, helps to keep things balanced. We need to acknowledge everyone has weaknesses as well as strengths (that means *you* too!). When you have healthy self-esteem, it is like being resilient — it doesn't mean you won't have times where you experience low self-esteem, but it does mean you will be less likely to 'buy into' it than you normally would. Situations may still be encountered that could be deemed 'at risk'; however your response when you have healthy self-esteem is more likely to be more helpful and positive — how you cope with them is likely to be different.

Let's look at this model of healthy self-esteem:

Chapter 2 Healthy Self-esteem

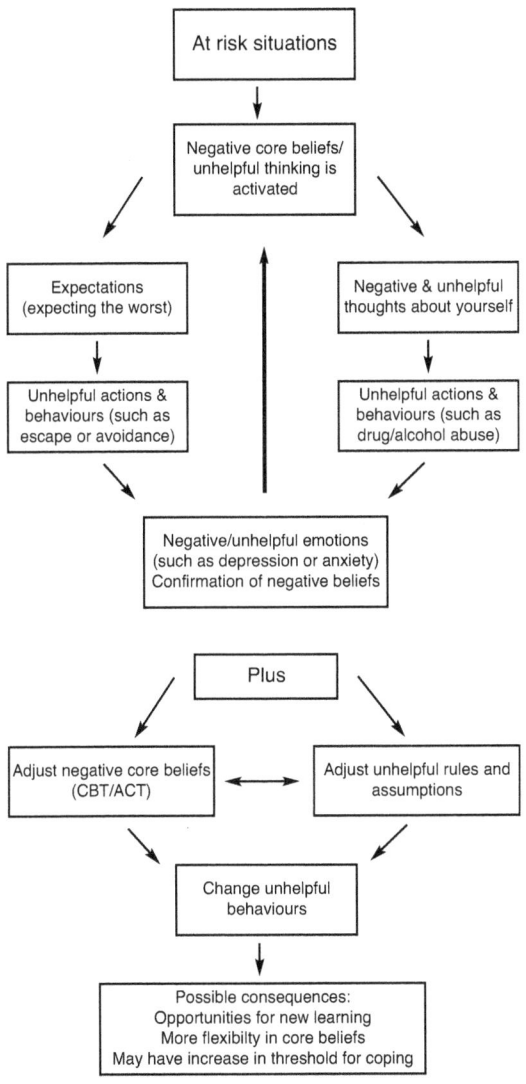

You can build healthy self-esteem by developing a record of 'positive qualities'. Some suggestions include:

- three good things you have experienced every day
- your achievements
- your positive characteristics
- the challenges you've overcome
- your talents or skills
- your positive attributes
- what others say they like about you.

If you are struggling to come up with a list of healthy self-esteem qualities and characteristics, here are a few self-descriptors to get you started:

- reliable
- organised
- determined
- funny
- friendly
- loved
- good friend
- good listener
- artistic
- charitable
- considerate
- creative
- strong
- good-humoured.

To apply this growing self-esteem to everyday experiences, you can help yourself by assessing your thoughts and feelings as you experience situations that might be triggers for negative self-esteem.

Ask yourself:
- Is this realistic?
- Is there evidence to support or go against my evaluations?
- Is it helpful?
- Are these facts or just opinions?
- Is there another way of viewing this situation?
- Are there other perspectives I could take?
- What would I suggest to others going through this?

It can also help to ask yourself and identify:
- How am I being self-critical?
- In what way am I evaluating myself?
- Am I putting myself down? If so, how?
- What am I experiencing right now?
- What is my self-talk like now?
- What is my self-talk like in this situation?

Unrealistic Expectations

As you may well already know, life sometimes throws us a curveball. Things don't always go as planned, even if we have worked hard to prepare for events meticulously. Sometimes our expectations can also be unrealistic, as well as the expectations others place on us.

So how do you deal with unrealistic expectations? You could try to ask yourself:

- Are these facts or just opinions from myself or others that I believe are true?
- Is there any evidence to support these expectations?

- Are these expectations realistic?
- Are these expectations helpful?

And remember...

Thoughts are just words – stories our mind tells us.
They are not always true.

Chapter 3

Mindfulness

You may be shocked to know that we spend just under 50 per cent of our time ruminating about the past or trying to predict (all too often with catastrophic imaginings!) the future. Being mindful helps stop you from getting caught up or 'buying into' all the things from the past or future that are obviously outside your control. It keeps you in the present moment, the here-and-now.

An example of how to practice being mindful is using the IMPROVE approach, a popular strategy from dialectical behaviour therapy (DBT).

IMPROVE is an acronym that stands for:

- Imagery — use imagery or imagination to visualise yourself in a beautiful place that makes you feel relaxed and at peace.
- Meaning —find the meaning in what you are doing. Why are you doing it? What do you want to accomplish by doing it?
- Pray or Practice —if you like to pray, you can use prayer to help ground yourself and/or help to ease the situation. Similarly, practice can be used to

improve your skills of mindfulness and not 'buying into' all the negative thoughts and feelings.
- Relax — engaging in an activity that is safe, healthy, and legal but helps you feel relaxed.
- One thing in the moment — focus on one thing at once, rather than trying to multitask. If you try to do too much, you'll likely end up not accomplishing anything.
- Vacation — if you are unable to physically take a vacation, perhaps try a 'staycation' or just some time out from worrying about everything. You could even try short dedicated 'worry' times rather than worrying all day.
- Encouragement — Surround yourself with people who support you — and while you are at it, use encouragement to motivate and reward yourself too!

Mindful meditation has also been shown to be the best coping skill to push past rumination (where you go over and over the same thoughts) — even slightly better than relaxation exercises.

Another mindfulness technique you might like to try is 'urge surfing'. This technique can help you move through an emotional experience without letting the urge take over or giving into it. To do this, you need to:
- Identify your urge (e.g., to eat, yell, throw something, buy into a negative thought).
- Locate your urge (e.g., is it in your stomach, chest, your head, or fists).
- Breathe through it (e.g., take deep breaths rather than short, shallow breaths). Focus on your urge as

a physical part of your body and direct your breathing to that area, imagining each outbreath as letting go of that urge.

While there are many ways to be mindful, sometimes the simplest strategies can get the best results. I personally love to sit with my eyes closed and just notice all the different sounds I can hear. It's amazing the number of things I can hear when I pay my attention to just listening — all the different birds I can hear, motorbikes, cars, the traffic on the highway, planes and helicopters, the wind, the pergola roof creaking, my dog walking around, the cat meowing to go outside, my breath — the list goes on!

One psychological therapy approach with great mindfulness strategies for coping is acceptance and commitment therapy (ACT, typically pronounced as the word 'act' rather than 'A-C-T'). (See chapter 14 for a brief overview of ACT.) ACT was developed around 30 years ago by Steven C. Hayes and colleagues. It helps you become aware of your automatic reactions by assisting you to think and feel what you are internally processing at the moment, rather than assuming what you are thinking and feeling. Fundamentally, the acronym of ACT can be described as:

- A = Accept your feelings and thoughts and be in the present moment.
- C = Choose a direction you value to move yourself forward.
- T = Take action toward that valued direction.

Practising mindfulness is a major focus of ACT which views mindfulness as a vital part of wellbeing, describing it as paying attention with curiosity, flexibility, and openness.

Some of the easiest mindfulness strategies I have found are to:

- Look around your environment and name or notice all the things (or limit it to five or ten things) you can see.
- Be quiet for a moment and notice all the things (or limit it to five or ten things) you can hear.
- Be quiet for a moment and notice all the things (or limit it to five or ten things) you can taste, smell, or touch.
- Notice your breath and imagine your stomach inflating like a balloon on the inhale and deflating on the exhale.
- Focus on your breathing — just notice the breath coming in through your nostrils and flowing out through your mouth.

If you have your own mindfulness strategies (there are seriously so many to choose from!) and they are safe, healthy, and legal, feel free to use them instead of any of the suggestions noted here. Try and incorporate at least 10–20 minutes of mindfulness into your daily routine as best you can — often, it can be helpful in the morning before you get stuck into your day, as it can help to put you in the right 'frame of mind' and set your day on a positive track. Some people find it helpful to practice mindfulness in the evening before they go to bed so they can switch off and calm down before going to sleep.

Find a strategy that works for you.

Chapter 4

Changing Careers

To some, a career may be nothing more than 'a job' — getting up, going to work, coming home — then repeating this the next workday. For others, a career can also feel like a life purpose, a mission, or a calling. When you find your ideal career, it can feel like a dream come true — but it also doesn't always stay that way. The novelty can begin to wear off over time, and you can be left questioning your career choices once again.

Changing careers can be a big step, and for some of us, it can also be life changing. Let's just say for me, it definitely was. Please indulge me a little while I share a bit of my own career journey.

For me personally, it took over a decade of working in different jobs before I really found what it was that I wanted to do when I grew up. Having left school at the age of 15 with no school qualifications, I was thrown into the workforce quickly. My first job was working as a mailroom clerk for a large organisation in Auckland City, New Zealand. I was very eager to learn and soon embraced the position, always willing to take on extra tasks and educate myself on as much as I could. I soon got a promotion to a branch office as a typist, another job I really enjoyed. After 12 months my parents chose to relocate back to the United Kingdom (where I was born), so I left that job and took up a casual role as a dental nurse in the UK for a few months before we moved to Australia in 1986. I was 17 years old at the time and very ambitious, searching for the 'perfect' job — even though I wasn't quite sure what that job was.

Once we settled on the Gold Coast (Queensland), I applied for a few vet nursing jobs, but was offered a casual position dental nursing instead. Let's just say I wasn't cut out to be a dental nurse, so I found other roles in administrative positions, working across healthcare, hospitality, private enterprise, and retail. It was in my role as Executive Assistant to the Centre Manager at a large shopping centre where I really started to question my career. I spoke to many of my colleagues and bosses about studying 'something', but nothing really seemed to appeal to me. That was until I read a book one day and the author was a psychologist — after reading about the work she did I realised becoming a psychologist was exactly what I was looking to become!

Once I graduated from university, completed my two-year internship, and became fully registered as a psychologist, I still didn't completely feel professionally satisfied. It wasn't until a life-changing discussion with a locum veterinarian that I really knew what my purpose was. I observed firsthand the toll on wellbeing and mental health that the unique stresses of the veterinary profession produced. I chose to research this at doctoral level from 2009 to 2016. Completing my doctoral studies and working exclusively with the veterinary profession and industry, I finally felt 'professionally complete'. I knew this was my calling. Yet it hasn't all been easy-sailing, and things didn't just fall into place for me. Those initial few years after graduating with my EdD were tough, and there were times I felt like walking away from it all. But I guess I did inherit some of the stubborn qualities from my parents and I kept plugging away at it and persevered. My instincts told me to stick with it, which I obviously did — and, while I wouldn't say doors swung open for me (often they creaked open reluctantly and slowly!), they definitely opened. The rest, they say, is history. It hasn't been easy, and yes there are quite a lot of times where I feel taken for granted, used, and unappreciated. But my mission is strong, and my determination is stronger — as is my resilience.

My point here is that I believe we all have a life purpose, something we want to stand for and make a difference in. Often though, I do feel that many people don't find this — either because they don't believe it will happen, or they give up when the going gets tough. One of my favourite quotes (from American author and former spiritual teacher Doreen Virtue) is 'don't give up right before the miracle occurs'. At times it feels like more of a mantra, but it is a great reminder to us all don't you think?

Particularly where careers are concerned, there are plenty of things you can do to help you identify your career options and set goals to try and accomplish them. The idea of setting goals is to give us something to aim for, something we can accomplish. Goals can also help in providing us with a sense of direction. However, our goals need to be SMART for them to be more realistic and achievable. SMART goals also keep us accountable — if our goals are open-ended, they may never be achieved.

SMART stands for:

S pecific

M easurable

A chievable

R ealistic

T ime-based.

Remember, if they are not SMART then they may not happen.

Working with someone who has experience in career counselling and guidance can be a good first step when contemplating a career change. When I first graduated from university, I relocated to Canberra in the Australian Capital Territory to start an internship as a Rehabilitation Consultant, working in occupational rehabilitation. As a provisional psychologist at the time, a lot of my clients ('cases') had psychological injuries, and not just physical injuries. One of the duties in this role required me to undertake vocational assessments with my clients, which was one of the aspects of my job that I really enjoyed. Being able to help people who felt all hope had been lost because of their respective injuries — many whose dream job and career had literally just been shattered — and work with them to identify an often-brand new career (generally involving some kind of retraining) and seek employment in that field, was highly rewarding. It was a constant reminder to me not only of how life as we know it can change in the blink of an eye, but how resilient we can be, and how adaptive to change we have the capacity for. They used to say most people will have around 10 different jobs or careers in their lifetime, so it is more common than you may think.

One thing I do want to say is that I have heard many times that a lot of veterinarians feel they 'can't' change their career because they have invested so much time, energy, and money, into studying to become a vet. Sometimes they say they feel like a failure if they leave the profession, like they are giving up on it all. While I generally disagree that changing a career means you are a failure, I believe there are some people who choose a particular career for a certain purpose (maybe they are pressured into it, or think they will earn lots of money from it, or they like the status it represents, etc.) that just may not be suited to them. Or they expect it will be a dream job, but the reality and expectations are miles apart. It may also be that they have done the job but are simply ready for new experiences and challenges. And that's totally okay. I remember quite a few years ago having a wonderful long telephone chat with the noted researcher and vet Dr Brian McErlean. He pointed out that he gives 'permission' to veterinarians who want to leave the profession. I totally agree with Brian on this — sometimes people feel they need to be told it's okay to move to another job or profession. It doesn't always mean you can't go back to that profession; it just means you are making a change. In my opinion it is better to change career or role, than stick with something just because this is what you feel is expected of you and feel miserable, unhappy, lost, or unfulfilled.

One of the first steps I would encourage is to think of what is known as your 'transferable skills'. What are the skills, experience, and knowledge you have that you could transfer to another job? I worked with a lot of people who felt they had nothing to transfer. Some were cleaners or checkout operators, so in these cases we would break down the tasks of their roles. We could then start to identify lots of things they had experience in doing, such as customer service, money handling, good hygiene practices, knowledge of chemicals for cleaning, problem solving, using equipment, and so forth. What are the range of skills, knowledge, and experience you have gained from the jobs you have held in your career?

Going back to my experience in occupational rehabilitation, we used a hierarchy for returning people to work, and it's something I use whenever I am working or helping people in the process of examining their career choices:

- Same job — same employer
- Different job — same employer
- Same job — different employer
- Different job — different employer.

I find this to be helpful in getting people to think outside the box. What it means is your first option is staying in the same job with the same employer (i.e., this could be the role you are in right now if you are working). If that's no longer suitable for you, then explore if there are different jobs you could do with that same employer. If that is not an option, then look for other employers where you could continue to do the same job as you are now. Your last alternative is to find a completely different job with a new employer. So, imagine you are a veterinary nurse working for the fictitious *Dr Hamilton's Amazing Veterinary Clinic*. Is remaining in this role still viable or suitable for you? If not, then are there other jobs you could do such as administrative roles, leadership or management roles, marketing roles, business development roles, etc. If there are no possibilities here, then could you find another job as a veterinary nurse with a new employer? And if that is not an option, then finding a new career and job with a new employer — for example, perhaps as a medical secretary with the fictitious *Dr Hamilton's Amazing Medical Centre* or a retail assistant at *Dr Hamilton's Amazing Retail Outlet*.

Of course, there are also occupational search inventories that can be used to help identify suitable jobs, which may be available through career counsellors or psychologists working in this area. I have used several of these with clients over the years and found them to be a very helpful tool.

Another career tip is to look through a broad range of job advertisements (either through the newspaper, online sources, notice boards, organisation websites etc.) and see what jobs are being advertised. While this obviously gives you an idea of what is available, it can often also give you some ideas that you have never considered. I once had an occupational rehabilitation client who had worked in a particular profession but wanted a complete change of career — she just didn't know what it was. So, I suggested she grab the local paper (this is back in the day when most of the jobs were advertised in the Saturday paper, not online as they seem to be now) and peruse the listings. She saw a job as a property manager that totally appealed to her (but which she had never even thought of before) and ended up gaining the necessary qualifications to enable her to do this job. After this, she was offered a job that she absolutely loved.

They say that 80% of jobs are on the 'hidden' job market. This means that up to 80% of jobs may not be publicly advertised. Another approach to use is to break the job search down into geographical locations, or employer, or industry, and then start researching what is available. For example, if you want to work in a particular suburb or radius, then look at whatever jobs are available in that area and ascertain if any appeal to you. Or you may want to work for a particular employer such as *Dr Hamilton's Amazing Businesses* — have a look on their website or contact them to find out if they have any career vacancies. The other option is to look at industries — so if you want to work in the veterinary industry, start researching what type of roles exist in this profession.

Chapter 5

Setting Boundaries

Are you willing to work minutes, hours, days, weeks, months, or years outside of the scope of your work contract? Are you happy for people to yell at you, abuse you, insult you, treat you badly, or otherwise tell you what to do?

I'm guessing (or at least I hope!) the answer to these questions would be a sharp 'no' most of the time. But even though we may not want these things or be willing to do them, too many continue down this path — subsequently letting people abuse them, treat them badly, or take advantage of them.

An important self-care necessity is the ability to be able to set boundaries — not just in your personal life but at work too. I have seen people's non-verbal responses (aka their body language) when I talk to them about setting boundaries — for some people they seem quite taken aback as it may be that they have a sense of fear about doing so — such as 'what will the other person think', or 'what if I offend them?'. In these cases, though, I would ask you — how do YOU feel about people mistreating you, and how do YOU feel about being offended? Often, we tend to put other people's opinions and concerns ahead of our own, which is not always helpful.

What are boundaries?

Boundaries are like 'conditions' or 'rules' we set for how we are prepared to let other people treat us or behave towards us. Imagine a fence — it sets a boundary between one property and another, indicating that you may or may not go beyond that fence line. This is what we are referring to with our self-imposed boundaries of what we are prepared to tolerate from others.

It's important to recognise that boundaries are not always psychological — they can be physical too.

Why are boundaries so important?

If you don't have boundaries, it can send the message to another person or people that they can treat you however they like, without any consequences. It can indicate that you will tolerate what they will throw at you — the good, the bad, and the downright ugly. Obviously, this is not okay! It reminds me of something my mum said to me many years ago 'people can only treat you a certain way if you let them' — in other words, no one can make you feel bad or act a certain way unless you let them.

Having healthy boundaries can help with developing a sense of identity and autonomy, as well as the ability to maintain good mental and emotional health and the potential to avoid burnout. They should be part of our everyday self-care, just like brushing our teeth, having a shower, and other activities we undertake daily.

How do we set boundaries?

One of the first steps in setting boundaries is to identify exactly what they are for you — that is, what you are prepared to accept and put up with and what you're not. For this step, think about your 'yes', 'no's' and 'maybes':

- Yes — what are the things, events, or circumstances in your life that you can accept regarding your boundaries? This could be things like being okay with people calling you at 6.00 am to encourage you to get out of bed to go and watch the sunrise you have always wanted to watch or having your loved ones tell you their honest opinion about what they really think of the dinner you cooked last night, or not minding if your loved ones give you a hug.

- No — what are the things, events, or circumstances in your life that you are not able to accept regarding your boundaries? This may include things like people raising their voice or yelling at you, people making inappropriate comments or gestures towards you, being expected to work every weekend even though it's not in your work contract, or strangers wanting to give you a hug.

- Maybe — these are the things you may or may not be too concerned about or depend on the situation or person/s involved. For example, you may not mind if someone swears around you or raises their voice in general conversation, but if it is directed at you personally or gets abusive, you absolutely may mind! Sometimes you may be open to a stranger giving you a hug if you have been very upset and they show genuine concern and compassion, but other times it may be completely inappropriate.

Another way of identifying your boundaries is to consider your *values*. I think of values as those things you want to stand for — the things that give you meaning and purpose. They are actions you take to try and live your life in a way that enhances your wellbeing rather than increasing your suffering. I find that an easy way to identify your values is to reflect on everyday things that happen to you or around you. In broader terms, this is about asking deeper questions when something good or not-so-good happens. For example — when something happens and it makes you feel good, stop and ask yourself why it makes you feel good. Maybe it's a moment spent cuddling with your partner or looking into your dog's eyes and having a moment of connection. Why is this so good? Perhaps it reminds you of unconditional love — this can indicate that unconditional love is something you value. On the other hand, if something happens that leaves you feeling angry, upset, fearful, or some other not-so-good feeling, ask yourself why this makes you feel so bad. So, in a scenario where someone has just yelled at you for something and you feel bad as a result, perhaps it means you don't like being accused of things you didn't do, or you find their behaviour aggressive or rude. This could indicate that you don't value these things — so what you do value is honesty, respect, and treating other people with kindness.

When you know what your values are (and I'm a firm believer we all have values; otherwise we wouldn't feel good or bad about different things — it's just that not everyone has taken the opportunity to drill down and identify what they are), it can become easier to identify why you feel the way you do. It also can remind you that these are the things you absolutely will or will not compromise on or accept — which brings it back to your boundaries.

Once you have identified what your values and boundaries are, take a moment to reflect on why they are so important to you. Do they help you feel more empowered, loved, respected, admired, validated, or some other feeling? What benefits do you notice or hope to notice once you start enforcing your boundaries? Next comes the part where you need to start enforcing them — but how?

This is where effective communication and assertiveness skills come in. Being able to communicate and assert yourself and your boundaries is going to be crucial if you want to enforce your boundaries. Think about how many conversations are misconstrued, or how many people misinterpret a text message or email. In my private practice I have worked with a lot of couples undergoing relationship counselling. Most of these couples had lost touch with how to communicate with each other either assertively, respectively, or both. Some of them wouldn't communicate at all, which often exacerbated the problem as this could lead to all sorts of scenarios in the other partner's mind!

There are three main types of communication:

- verbal (speech)
- non-verbal (e.g., facial expressions, body language, gestures)
- written (e.g., texts, emails, social media).

Verbal Communication

Verbal communication is that which is spoken — it includes things such as:

- conversations with people that are face-to-face or via telephone
- listening to things such as the television or radio
- conversations through media such as FaceTime, Skype, Zoom etc. Using verbal communication is a way to communicate your ideas and thoughts using words or in turn to listen to the words being spoken. While this communication is occurring, you need to be mindful of how your language is also expressing both *connotation* and *denotation*.

Connotation in verbal communication refers to the subjective or emotional meaning of words being used when someone is expressing themselves, rather than the *denotation* — the objective accepted dictionary meaning. As an example, you might talk about 'change' in a family's normal routine as a possible cause for the onset of new behaviour in a pet. This would be a normal and helpful step in trying to solve a client issue. However the client, due to their own unique experiences, may attach negative emotions to the word 'change'. This might result in the client reacting in a defensive way when in fact there is no intention to be accusative or confronting in any way.

Non-verbal Communication

This method of communication involves all the other cues that come about within spoken communication. Since we do not robotically enunciate words from a fixed speaker,

these non-verbal cues are a significant part of communication. Non-verbal communication includes:
- our gestures and facial expressions
- how we present ourselves / our appearance
- body language
- our behaviour
- sign language
- emails, letters, text messages and other correspondence
- social media content.

Non-verbal communication gives you the opportunity to communicate attitudes, emotions, and affect, but it is important not to make assumptions about the connotation behind the message when you are interpreting it. It also adds a layer of complexity to verbal communication in the following ways:
- it may contradict verbal messages (e.g., saying 'I'm fine' but the body language shows otherwise)
- it can be ambiguous (e.g., raising eyebrows or shrugging shoulders can send different messages)
- it conveys emotion (e.g., touching someone's arm or facial expressions such as smiling)
- it is multi-channelled (e.g., facials, voice, tone, body language). When you think about different ways of communicating non-verbally, it is important to consider the ways in which your message could be interpreted. As an example, consider the statement 'how are you!'. Based on this sentence, you could interpret this a few ways — the first is that the sender may not have heard from you in a while and could

be asking excitedly 'OMG how are you!', or it could be interpreted as something a little cranky like 'hmmm, so how are you!'.

The way in which we communicate non-verbally is obviously crucial as it can be very easy for our message to be misconstrued. It is important to note how you are feeling while communicating to ensure you are being as congruent as you can. If you are stressed or pressured about a matter unrelated to the communication you are having, you need to try and not let that intrude on your non-verbal signals. Try and stay in the moment. Giving a simple instruction to a staff member after being blind-sided by a client complaining about the cost of treatment for their pet can quickly become loaded with inappropriate emotion unless you have given yourself time (and a few deep breaths) to regather your focus.

Similarly, when listening to someone while our body language conveys that we need to be somewhere else will likely be noticed and interpreted in a way we are not in control of.

Written Communication

Not so long ago in history, people wrote letters to each other as the main way to stay in contact for either friendship or business. Nowadays, we tend to think that written communication is mostly about formal communication (excluding notes passed around class). Yet much more casual communication between friends, family, colleagues and even clients occurs in a written context via texts, tweets, message services and emails, even though in our minds we are 'speaking' to the other person. The use of acronyms and emojis with a shared understanding of their meaning helps convey emotional content along with the words but can only go so far. Without even the complexities of a voice to convey extra meaning, a quick typed text remains limited in the amount of subjective emotional content it can convey to the recipient. Therefore, it is important to ensure you double-check anything you send BEFORE you send it to make sure your communication is interpreted in the manner it is intended (as best you can).

Poor Communication

In my experience there are three common forms of poor communication that most often cause difficulties both at home and at work. It is important to see if you identify with any of these as either something you might be prone to doing or something you recognise in someone you regularly communicate with.

Passive Communication

Sometimes people may behave in a passive manner because they have low self-esteem, limited levels of confidence, or low self-respect. They may feel that they do not have the right to say something or feel a certain way or could even have the belief that no one will listen to them and therefore there is little point in speaking up. Passive people will generally shy away from conversations, look away, or say things like 'it doesn't matter', or 'it's not important', and may be very quiet, timid, and/or shy.

Passive-aggressive Communication

There are some people who act in a passive-aggressive way — this is where they may act both passively and aggressively at the same time. That is, they may act in an aggressive way by looking away while at the same time making a loud 'huff' or muttering something under their breath. Passive-aggressive people do not come straight out with aggressive behaviour, instead, it is conducted in a more passive way. They may choose to do this for several reasons — for example, they may wish to avoid confrontation by getting embroiled in a heated conversation, or they may feel their comments will not be listened to, or they may not feel confident enough to speak up directly.

Aggressive Communication
Aggressive people behave in a way that attempts to make others agree with them while having no regard for the other person's feelings or opinion. They tend to express their opinions and feelings in a manner that can be perceived as intimidating or bullying or in a way that attacks other people who may be communicating at the time. Underneath this behaviour tends to be the desire to 'win' and force other people to accept their viewpoint regardless.

Assertiveness

Although many people may think assertiveness and aggressiveness are the same things, they are not — and you certainly do not need to be aggressive to be assertive.

People who are assertive say what they would like to say and/or express themselves in a manner that is respectful to themselves and the other person/people. Assertive communication is the best way to communicate with others in difficult conversations, as it attempts to maintain a collaborative and positive approach to the discussion/s.

When acting in an assertive manner, you should maintain eye contact and ensure your body language is upright and confident (rather than slouched) to portray an image of confidence and assertiveness. You should always use 'I' statements rather than using accusatory comments (such as 'you did this' or 'you did that'), as this is an indication that you are taking responsibility for your own feelings, rather than blaming or accusing the other person. It also helps to reduce any potential retaliation from the other person, who is less likely to feel like they are being accused of something and less likely to respond defensively.

When communicating assertively you should:

1. state what the problem is
2. say how you feel
3. and then state how you would like the situation to be resolved.

Again, don't forget to replace 'you' with 'I' to take responsibility for your feelings and to remove any accusatory comments that could result in resentment and defensive behaviour.

Dealing With Difficult People

While it can be frustrating when other people don't act or respond in the way we would like, we need to remember that their behaviour is outside of our control. But that can also leave us wondering why some people are seemingly 'difficult' (be mindful though that you could be perceiving someone as difficult just because they don't agree with you — that doesn't necessarily mean they are difficult; it means they have a different opinion).

It is often said there are two sides to the story — in fact, there's three! Yours, theirs, and the truth. For conflict to resolve itself amicably, it is imperative that both parties are heard. Being able to communicate assertively and with a genuine desire to resolve the situation is crucial.

There could be several reasons why people are 'difficult' — here are a few:

- they are stressed, worried, or anxious about things at work or in their personal lives and are consumed by their own emotions
- they do not realise their behaviour is offensive and rude
- they do not know how to communicate effectively
- they may feel they have been treated rudely by you or other workmates
- they do not feel heard or listened to
- they could just be a rude person full-stop!

Remember:

- other people's behaviour is outside of your control
- you can only control, and be responsible for, your own behaviour
- no-one can force you to act or feel a particular way unless you allow it to happen
- Opinions are like heads — everyone has one. However your opinion should be the most important to you.

Quick Tips

Sometimes you need to remember some quick tips in the heat of the moment. Here's a few of my favourites:

Stop, drop, and roll

To use an analogy of my good friend, US Attorney Debra Vey Voda-Hamilton, when faced with conflict we should stop, drop, and roll:

>STOP — how do I stop talking and listen?
>
>DROP — how do I drop the need to be right?
>
>ROLL — how do I let what the other party says roll off my back?

D.O.G.S

To make it easy to remember, you can also use my DOGS acronym:

>Drop your defensiveness
>
>Observe what is going on — be mindful rather than reactive
>
>Ground yourself — take a deep breath before you respond
>
>Support — make sure you seek support if you need it.

C.A.T.S

Or maybe you're a cat person:

>Compassion and care
>
>Appreciate the opportunity to listen and respond
>
>Trust yourself to act assertively
>
>Show you care and want to resolve the matter amicably.

Chapter 6

Stress

'Argghhh, I'm so stressed!' 'Darn, this job gets me so stressed out!' 'That customer gets me so stressed!' Do these words sound familiar?

Whereas stress used to seemingly be a taboo topic, it now seems to have become so commonplace that is nearly trendy! But stress is no joke. Sadly, it can be fatal.

What is stress?

Did you know that there is 'good' stress (called 'eustress') as well as 'bad' stress (called 'distress')? We need a certain amount of both the good and the bad stress to help keep us motivated. But too much distress can have fatal consequences, so being able to effectively manage stress is vital for our health and wellbeing. Imagine how it would feel to be as stress-free as possible. How would your life feel without stress (and even anxiety, depression, and/or burnout)? What would you be doing differently?

There are loads of things happening inside your body when you are feeling stressed. When you are stressed, your body goes into the 'fight or flight' response which releases stress hormones called cortisol and adrenaline that can cause a series of reactions that reduce digestion, turn off your immune system, increase your blood pressure, create tension in your muscles, and pauses growth. The fight or flight response evolved in humans to help us escape from danger. However, as we have evolved to a level where normal life is generally not full of deadly predators the fight or flight response works overtime as we perceive many different triggers as deadly threats — even while they may not be. This constant state of stress can take its toll on your body.

The Autonomic Nervous System

The autonomic nervous system has two parts, the *sympathetic nervous system* and the *parasympathetic nervous system*. The sympathetic nervous system is likened to an accelerator — or the 'fight or flight' response and prepares the body for impending activity in response to a threat.
The parasympathetic nervous system is likened to the brakes — or the 'rest and digest' response which slows the body down.

When the body senses a stressor (danger), it can cause a chain reaction whereby the brain signals the amygdala, part of the brain's limbic system, which has a primary role in processing decision-making and emotional responses, as well as memory. The amygdala then tries to figure out if the danger is real or not, and if it determines that it is, it sounds an alarm in the brain's command centre — the hypothalamus. It is the hypothalamus that switches on the fight or flight response. Once this happens the adrenal glands start to pump adrenaline (epinephrine) into the body, which pumps blood to the muscles, releases sugar in the bloodstream for energy to be able to escape, opens the airways ready for you to run, and causes the heart to beat faster. The next phase after this initial release of adrenaline has settled down is to release more hormones to keep the accelerator (sympathetic nervous system) firmly pressed until the perceived danger has gone. Once the sense of danger has passed, the parasympathetic nervous system kicks in and presses the brakes, subsequently turning off the stress reaction. Unfortunately, in today's busy life where many people are dealing with chronic stress, the body always assumes there is danger, resulting in the sympathetic nervous system being activated and the parasympathetic nervous system unable to step in.

Physiological Effects

When you are stressed in the short term, this stress can cause your heart to beat faster and harder, subsequently increasing the risk of heart attack, stroke, and high blood pressure (hypertension). There can also be an increased risk of inflammation throughout our body which can have a negative impact on cholesterol levels but also lead to a heart attack.

Over time, stress can tense our muscles, which can then lead to migraines and tension headaches. Even the experience of chronic pain following an injury can feel much worse. Blood sugar can also increase when we are stressed as the body pumps more sugar into our bloodstream to give us the energy to take flight. This can then lead to an increased risk of diabetes.

Our brain can also be impacted by the fight or flight response, which can affect our ability to learn new things and make new memories. As if this isn't enough, stress can also affect the reproductive system. For women, it can delay or shut down their monthly cycle and even worsen symptoms of PMS. Cortisol has also been known to negatively affect hormones such as oestrogen and progesterone. For men, the effects aren't that pleasant either, as it is known to also affect certain body parts negatively.

Chronic Stress

When we chronically overreact to people and events surrounding us, most of us feel like we are in a state of constant stress. This can indeed mean that we are suffering from an overload of cortisol. Cortisol is one of the stress hormones released when our bodies go into the 'fight or flight' response. High levels of cortisol and chronic stress have been associated with anxiety and depression, a weakened immune system, weight increases, and conditions such as heart disease and hypertension.

As well as being one of the hormones responsible for how our body responds to stress, cortisol also plays a role in regulating blood sugar levels, inflammation, metabolism, and immune responses. If our body continues to release cortisol when we are chronically stressed for a long period, it has been known to cause shrinkage in the size of the brain, impair long-term learning, kill brain cells, and influence disorders of emotion.

Sleep

The stress cycle can be fed into by a lack of sleep, which can impact your judgement, memory, and mood — which can be like a vicious cycle that makes you feel more susceptible to the effects of stress. Lack of sleep can affect your stress levels by lowering the threshold where you perceive stress. This means that if you have had a late night, you may be more likely to interpret certain situations as more stressful versus when you have had a good rest.

Another negative side-effect of a lack of sleep (less than seven hours sleep) is the effect on our hunger hormones — leptin and ghrelin. Leptin is the hormone that tells us we are full, but this decreases when we lack sleep. On the other hand, ghrelin — which is the hormone that signals to us that we are hungry — increases when we lack sleep.

Exercise

While we may have all heard about the many benefits of exercise, did you know that it can reduce cortisol and boost serotonin? Serotonin is a neurotransmitter and chemical that is best known for the role it plays in regulating mood. Increased happiness and lower levels of anxiety and depression are associated with higher levels of serotonin.

In a nutshell, exercise helps to produce more serotonin which can help to make us feel happier and less stressed. It can also help to decrease levels of circulating cortisol.

Our Imagination

Believe it or not, our imagination — or the ability to imagine the worst and ask, 'what if?' — can be behind a lot of the stress and worry in our lives. Being able to recognise this — and not 'buy into it' is crucial. Using strategies from accepted psychological theories such as Acceptance and Commitment Therapy (ACT) (See chapter

14 for a brief overview of ACT) or Cognitive Behaviour Therapy (CBT) may be helpful.

Workplace Stress

It is suggested that workplace stress is now the most widespread and common source of stress. There are reports that in over 50% of people reporting high levels of stress, financial issues and work problems are the most common.

Stress Management Strategies

Since we know that stress can have fatal consequences, being able to effectively manage it is vital for health and wellbeing. The good news though is that you can always try to turn things around and take a proactive, rather than reactive, approach. Research has shown that, despite age, taking steps to combat the effects of stress on the brain is effective — although generally, the younger you are when you take proactive steps to de-stress, the better.

While I have listed my top ten stress-busting strategies on the following pages, some quick tips are:

- exercise (which is said to help release tension in the muscles as well as breathing more deeply — not to mention releasing serotonin!),
- spending time with those you love and not being afraid to reach out for support,
- meditation (while you could engage in formal meditation activities, even prayer, deep breathing, or just focusing on calming words can help),
- flowing movements (such as tai chi or yoga, which is believed to help us breathe more deeply and slow

down our breath — with the bonus of helping to increase mental focus).

You may also find it helpful to think of using a traffic light approach to stress.

Red light — stop
This is the step where you stop and reflect on your stressors and your symptoms. Your stressors are the things that make or contribute to you feeling stressed, and your symptoms are the ways you feel when you are stressed — i.e., your stress response such as physical sensations, urges, thoughts, or actions.

Orange/amber light — reflect
Once you have recognised your stressors and symptoms, and you are identifying them in the moment, you can then identify all the options you have to intervene — as well as their potential consequences. In other words, if you act on the feelings and thoughts you are having, will you be happy about that in the long run? Will you be pleased with the consequences? You may also like to think of what has worked for you in the past or what didn't work so well, and keep these in mind when you choose how to proceed.

Green light — go
Now you have assessed all your opportunities and their associated potential consequences; ideally you want to choose an action/response that will be most helpful in the long run (not just the short term). This is the action step where you behave/respond in the way that you believe will bring you the best possible outcomes — those most aligned with your values. It may be helpful to remind

yourself that just because you are thinking it, it doesn't mean it's true — you are in control of how you choose to respond, not your thoughts.

To help you with further strategies to put in your psychological toolbox, here are my top ten stress-busting strategies that you can start using right now!

Stress Management Tip #1

Know your stressors. Learn to recognise the things that get you stressed (your 'stressors'). For example, if you know that catching a train full of crowded people to go to a concert where you'll be in the mosh pit is going to get you totally stressed out, then consider if it is really a good idea. If you really want to attend the concert and travel by train, then develop appropriate strategies for helping you to acknowledge that you will likely be feeling stressed and how you can effectively cope with this (see tip #9).

If work is one of your stressors, try using your commute home from work to reflect on your day and think of one thing that was good, the choices you made that contributed to these good things, and ways you can make good choices for future events.

Stress Management Tip #2

Recognise your symptoms. Being able to recognise the symptoms you feel when you are stressed can help you take a more proactive role in combating stress. Some common symptoms include things such as a tense stomach, feeling nauseous, being irritable and short-tempered, breathing more rapidly, sweating, over-thinking, feeling powerless, headaches, and having an increased heart rate. If you recognise the symptoms early on, you can become more proactive in dealing with them and identify opportunities for intervention, such as identification of thought distortions and exploring healthier ways to respond.

Stress Management Tip #3

Practice mindfulness. Mindfulness is essentially about 'being in the moment' or the 'here and now'. When you are mindful, you are not caught up in the past or future — you are dealing with this very moment, right here, right now. Check the chapter on coping strategies for some mindfulness tips.

Stress Management Tip #4

Practice relaxation. Relaxation isn't just about sitting down and doing nothing! Relaxation is whatever you do that helps you to feel relaxed — so for some people, this could be different things. Some common forms of relaxation include meditation, surfing, gardening, dancing, reading, art, singing, different forms of exercising, stroking an animal, listening to music, watching television or internet videos, colouring-in, journalling, reflecting, laughing, and sitting quietly. (My golden rule is that it needs to be safe, healthy, and legal though!)

Stress Management Tip #5

Remember to socialise. For many people, surrounding ourselves with supportive friends and family can be a great form of stress relief. Laughing releases endorphins (the feel-good chemicals) and helps us to de-stress in the long run. Being with family and friends can also distract us from whatever our minds are caught up in and help us to focus on something else in the short term.

Stress Management Tip #6

Try for a good work/life balance. Developing a good work-life balance is essential to our health and wellbeing. Work/life balance isn't necessarily about 50% of your time at home and 50% of your time at work — it is about finding a balance that works for you.

Stress Management Tip #7

Develop SMART goals. Sometimes we can get stressed because we do not have SMART goals. SMART goals are **s**pecific, **m**easurable, **a**chievable, **r**ealistic, and time-based. When our goals are SMART, we are in a much better position to achieve them, thus lessening the extra stress of failing.

Stress Management Tip #8

Learn assertiveness skills. Learn how to speak up and say no! When you are assertive, you can get your message across in a respectful manner — being respectful to yourself and the other person. Being assertive is NOT about being aggressive or passive — it is about confidently and respectfully taking ownership of how you are feeling when a particular thing happens by making 'I' statements and stating what you would like as the outcome.

Stress Management Tip #9

Develop personal coping strategies. Stress is a very real part of life for all of us. What stresses one person is not necessarily going to stress another person, and therefore we are all going to experience stress in different ways. Being able to develop coping strategies APPROPRIATE to who you are is essential to managing stress and enabling a sense of wellbeing. I recommend strategies derived from ACT and Positive Psychology.

Stress Management Tip #10

Seek professional support. If you feel like stress has control of you, it is essential to take appropriate action and do something about it. Being proactive rather than reactive is crucial! If you do not feel like you have appropriate (and by this, I mean healthy, legal, and safe!) strategies, I highly recommend you seek professional help. Speaking with your GP may help for general advice or a recommendation to an appropriate professional. An experienced psychologist is a great way of taking action, as they can generally help you to develop your own appropriate coping strategies to combat stress.

To summarise this chapter, remember that it is better to be proactive rather than reactive. Taking small steps each day can lead to big changes! Don't be afraid to put yourself first, and remember that if something doesn't feel right — speak up or walk away. Likewise, don't say 'yes' if you really mean 'no' — doing so could create more stress.

Chapter 7

Dealing with Anxiety

Have you ever felt worried about something that just won't go away? Has that worry kept you awake at night and made you feel agitated, irritable, and even nauseous, flustered, or light-headed? Chances are, you may have experienced anxiety.

Anxiety can be described as experiencing intrusive, recurring, and specific fears that you know are not realistic or rational. Experiencing anxiety is quite normal, and when it is 'functional' (i.e., moderate and sometimes high), it can be quite helpful. For example, it may assist in improving performance when the demands of the situation are consistent (such as preparing for an important meeting or interview). However, severe anxiety (which could be described as dysfunctional) is not helpful.

Anxiety and stress are not necessarily the same thing, even though some of the symptoms may be the same. Typically, I would describe stress as symptoms that occur in relation to a particular situation or concern, and it has been known as a precursor to anxiety. For example, you may feel stressed about getting all your jobs done by Sunday evening so you can relax and watch your favourite show before going to bed. Anxiety is typically more related to a fear of something, which may not always be realistic. For example, you might feel anxious about an upcoming meeting with the boss and what that may entail, and you worry that you may get reprimanded or sacked.

Common symptoms

Generally, the symptoms of anxiety can be broken down into three areas:

- *psychological* — such as:
  - worry
  - obsessive thinking
  - excessive fear
  - catastrophic thinking
- *behavioural* — such as:
  - avoidance of different situations which contribute to your feelings of anxiety (study, work, social activities etc.)
- *physical* — such as:
  - racing heart
  - hyperventilation (quick breathing)
  - panic attacks (see subsequent symptoms)
  - feeling irritable, tense, wound-up, and/or restless
  - tightness of the chest
  - feeling dizzy, light-headed, faint
  - tingling, flushes, chills.

Chapter 7 Dealing with Anxiety

Anxiety disorders

For some people though, the anxiety may develop into something more, becoming an anxiety disorder. While you may have heard of some of them before, it may surprise you to know there are several types of anxiety disorders:

- panic disorder
- agoraphobia
- obsessive-compulsive disorder
- social phobia
- generalised anxiety disorder
- specific phobia.

Let's take a closer look at each of these.

Panic attack/disorder

This disorder can be categorised by unexpected and recurrent panic attacks and subsequent concerns about the implications of the panic attacks themselves, that is, worrying about having another panic attack.

Some of the symptoms of a panic attack include:

- shortness of breath
- pounding heart
- dizziness or light-headedness, faintness
- tingling feet or fingers
- tightness or pain in the chest
- trembling or shaking
- muscle tension
- dry mouth
- nausea/butterflies

65

- blurred vision
- hot or cold flushes
- desire to flee (fight/flight)
- fear of dying, losing control, going mad
- difficulty speaking or gathering thoughts.

Agoraphobia

Agoraphobia is when a person feels anxious about situations where they may find it difficult or embarrassing to escape or where help may not be available in the event of experiencing a panic attack or panic-like symptoms.

It is generally a complication resulting from panic disorder. Symptoms include avoidance of situations such as:

- travelling on trains, cars, buses, planes
- being in crowded areas
- being on a bridge
- being home alone
- being in an elevator.

Obsessive-compulsive disorder (OCD)

Intrusive and unpleasant thoughts which can be hard to control can be a result of obsessive-compulsive disorder. Obsessive thoughts can lead to compulsive rituals that are uncontrollable. What some people don't realise is that you can have one without the other — that is, you can have the obsessions without the compulsions and vice versa.

Symptoms include:

- difficulties with unwanted, persistent, intrusive thoughts and images

- overwhelming and persistent urges or compulsions to perform specific rituals (behaviours)
- anxiety
- depression.

Social phobia
Social phobia can occur when you feel overly anxious about being evaluated or scrutinised by others, you worry about doing something embarrassing in front of others, or you are overly concerned about offending someone in a normal social exchange.

The anxiety this causes can lead to avoidance of situations.

Symptoms include:

- anxiety and even panic attacks caused by exposure to the feared situation
- recognition that the fear is excessive and irrational
- persistent and marked fear of being scrutinised by others in different performance or social situations (with the fear involving behaving in ways that would be humiliating or embarrassing)
- marked distress during exposure due to the sense of fear
- avoidance of the situation.

Generalised anxiety disorder (GAD)
Excessive and persistent worry about different and generalised areas of life such as health, finances, family, or job can be related to GAD. A person with GAD would likely

be anxious or worried about anything — that is, it is not usually related to a specific thing or situation.

Symptoms include:
- muscular tension
- trembling
- irritability
- restlessness or nervousness
- sweating
- light-headed or dizzy
- shortness of breath
- trouble falling or staying asleep
- palpitations
- poor concentration
- frequent urination
- depressed mood
- easily fatigued
- hypervigilance.

Specific phobia
Irrational and persistent fear of situations or objects, usually leading to avoidance of these things, can be typical of specific phobia. This can include things such as a fear of insects, heights, snakes, closed spaces, water, flying, blood, or injury.

Symptoms include:
- pounding heart / accelerated heart rate
- faintness or light-headedness
- sweating

- difficulty breathing
- trembling.

While some of these disorders and symptoms can sound scary, and while some people may need the help of an experienced mental health professional qualified to treat people with their symptoms, there are some relatively quick and easy things you can do to try and keep anxiety at a manageable level:

- deep breathing — refer to the chapter on relaxation for specific deep breathing techniques
- as you breathe, release the unhelpful thoughts on the exhale
- if you are hyperventilating or having a panic attack, try to hold your breath for a few seconds and then release it slowly through the mouth to effectively 'reset' the breathing. Then inhale through the nose slowly and exhale through the mouth slowly to regulate the breathing
- slow down — if you talk, walk, and do everything at breakneck speed, slow it down a little (make sure you're being safe though!)
- practice regular relaxation
- reality check or is it f.e.a.r (False Evidence Appearing Real)
- mindfulness — connect with your senses
- know your triggers
- consider reputable apps from reliable sources such as *Calm* or *Insight Timer*
- use evidence-based strategies such as ACT or CBT.

In summary — remember to slow down and breathe! It is important to recognise what is within your control and what isn't, so practice mindfulness regularly to enable it to become an automatic process. It can also be helpful to acknowledge the thought/feeling and choose to respond in a less-anxious manner.

Thoughts become things, so make sure you are not 'buying into' and believing every thought that comes into your head.

And remember — just because you are thinking it, it doesn't mean it is true!

Chapter 8

Dealing with Depression

Depression is more than just feeling down or having 'the blues', which tend to be short-term. Depression is also different to grief — while the symptoms can feel very similar when we are bereaved, these feelings are generally a healthy response to loss. Depression involves feelings that are more long-lasting and are accompanied by emotional, cognitive, and physical symptoms that significantly negatively affect a person's day-to-day life.

Despite what people may say, depression is not something a person can just 'snap out of', nor can they just 'pull themselves together' as others may think.

So, what causes depression?

Historically, there are thought to be several related factors that can lead to depression such as:

- personality types (typically perfectionist personality types, those experiencing high anxiety levels, and those sensitive to criticism)
- biochemical (a chemical imbalance combined with mood-regulating neurotransmitters that are not working properly)

- hereditary (having a genetic predisposition — not a guarantee but can be a higher risk)
- stress (experiencing stressful events such as job loss, financial loss, relationship loss).

Some people question if it is all in their head, especially if others accuse them of 'being dramatic' or 'attention-seeking'. If you are one of these people wondering if it is all in your head, the answer is no! There is new research emerging regarding the gut-brain axis and its effect on mood (aka the food/mood connection). Most of our happy chemicals (neurotransmitters) are formed in the gut. In fact, around 95% of serotonin (the happy chemical) and around 50% of dopamine (the pleasure chemical) resides in the gastrointestinal tract. If there are issues with the gut, it can play havoc with these neurotransmitters and their pathway to the brain via the gut-brain axis, and in turn, the pathway back to the gut.

There is also a strong connection between the food we eat and our mood, which I think is good news because it means that if our diet is playing an instrumental role in our mood, it could be identified (and potentially corrected) relatively easily.

Symptoms of depression

Some of the symptoms of depression can include:

- **Loss of interest in tasks and routines.** It is common for people experiencing depression to no longer enjoy activities they once did, which can result in a lack of achievement and positive emotion — subsequently affecting people around them.

- **Changes in sleeping patterns.** People experiencing depression may notice changes in their sleep patterns with increased insomnia, disrupted sleep, or excessive sleeping. Disrupted sleep or a lack of sleep can create issues with our hunger hormones (leptin and ghrelin) and contribute to weight issues. People can also experience changes in the production of other hormones, especially cortisol and melatonin, which further interrupt sleep behaviour, setting up a vicious cycle of poor sleep.
- **Irritability, fatigue, and agitation.** Such emotions are commonly experienced by the depressed person. There could be frustrations due to the lack of support they feel, lack of understanding of others, or their perceived lack of progress in 'getting better'. Often the depressed person is told to 'snap out of it' or to 'pull yourself together'. It is not that simple. These emotions can contribute to increased levels of stress — in turn resulting in increased cortisol levels, which can then affect sleep…and so the cycle continues.
- **Hopelessness.** Depressed people often describe how they are feeling by using the analogy of a black hole they are unable to climb out of. They may feel hopeless — particularly if they feel others don't understand how they are feeling. Unfortunately this feeling of hopelessness can lead to suicidal thoughts as a 'way out' of the pain they are experiencing.
- **Worrying (ruminating) and negative thinking.** Negative thinking and worrying are commonly observed in people experiencing depression. They may worry because they don't have the answer to

the problem/s they are trying to solve. Yet the more they worry and 'buy into' seemingly endless concerns about a problem, the more they can convince themselves of their perceived hopelessness.

- **Suicidal ideation.** Sadly, some depressed people feel the only solution to their continued depressive feelings is to end the thoughts by ending their life. They see suicide as an end to their suffering and do not always realise it is final if they complete their suicide attempt. They are thinking irrationally — choosing a permanent solution to a temporary problem. When a person is thinking irrationally, they are generally not making healthy decisions or choices.

Treatment

Generally, there are two major treatment forms for depression:

- psychological therapy
- medication.

These two forms of treatment may also be used together as a combination treatment. As with anxiety, some people (depending on the level and seriousness of their depression) may need professional support from a qualified mental health practitioner to assist with their symptoms. However, there are a few things you can do which may be helpful:

- Speak up to your family and/or friends and reach out for support.
- Increase your levels of engagement in pleasurable activities and try to incorporate these into each day.

- Increase your level of physical activity — get out in nature and/or exercise to endeavour to get the endorphins (natural chemicals) activated. Engaging in some form of exercise is beneficial to your mood, even if it's only walking around your garden.
- Set aside 'worry time'. Dedicate a particular time each day (not too long) to 'worry' rather than worrying all day, every day.
- Use evidence-based coping strategies such as ACT, CBT, and positive psychology to better your mood.
- Practice the three good things approach. Each day, make a list of three good things about yourself and things you have done, seen, or heard.
- Try journalling. Keeping a journal of your thoughts helps to get them out of your head and onto a page you can close.
- Keep a gratitude diary of all the things you are grateful for.
- Engage in safe, healthy, and legal relaxation activities.
- Periodically stop and take notice of your thoughts — what are they telling you?
- Don't believe everything that your mind is telling you.
- Practice good sleep hygiene and aim for at least eight hours each night.
- Make use of crisis lines or speak to a mental health professional when your depressive feelings get too strong.

- Remember the value of social support. Talk with a trusted friend, family member, or colleague about how you are feeling.

In summary then, when dealing with depressive feelings, relax and breathe to calm yourself down (especially if irritable). Recognise what is within your control and what isn't, and practice mindfulness regularly, so it becomes an automatic process.

Thoughts become things, so make sure you are not 'buying into' your depressive thoughts and believing everything that comes into your head. Just because you are thinking something, it doesn't mean it is true! Finally, just because you may be experiencing depression at the present time, it doesn't mean it is going to be permanent.

Chapter 9

Coping with Grief

Grief. Quite frankly, I think it sucks. But unfortunately, as humans, it is something we will generally all experience at some time. For a lot of us, our first experience with grief may be the loss of a pet or grandparent. I have met people in their 40s who have not lost anyone close to them, which I think is incredibly lucky. Sadly, I had my first notable experience with grief in primary school when we lost our beautiful collie dog, Shane.

But before I talk more about grief, I do want to point out that grief isn't just related to the loss of a person or pet. It can also be related to the loss of an important job, a significant relationship, or even treasured possessions. Put simply, grief can happen when we lose something or someone we value or have a special connection with.

For those of you working in professions where grief is common (such as the veterinary professionals I work with, but it can also include other professions such as medical and health professionals, first responders, emergency services workers, and so forth), I think it is worth taking the time to consider how this grief impacts you and your wellbeing. Especially for those exposed to death and dying regularly — it can certainly be taxing and make you question your own mortality. Not always a pleasant thing to contemplate!

There have been many books written on the topic of grief, but one of the most memorable things I remember being taught by one of my psychology supervisors is that 'we don't counsel people in grief — it's a process they have to go through'. I have found that over the years of working with thousands of clients, the majority of those grieving just want to normalise what they are feeling — particularly those who haven't been through a grief process before. In saying that though, there have been a couple of clients where the grief was unresolved and became what we call 'complicated grief', and this is where some counselling strategies were used.

Personally and professionally, I follow the Elisabeth Kubler-Ross model of grief. Dr Kubler-Ross was a renowned psychiatrist and quite a remarkable woman. (If you ever want to know more about her story, she has several books and has even been interviewed by Oprah Winfrey — her story is quite inspiring.) Dr Kubler-Ross researched death and dying extensively and noticed how her dying patients went through similar stages. She spoke about five stages of grief — shock/denial, anger/rage followed by grief and pain, bargaining, depression, and acceptance. Let's have a quick look at these stages.

Shock/denial

This is that first stage of grief where it seems surreal and like it cannot possibly be true. For example, you go into shock initially, and then the denial comes. You expect your loved one to call you at the same time each day as they used to, or you expect they will walk through the door any minute. Then the reality hits you that you won't see them in the physical world ever again. When it is no longer feasible to be in denial, anger becomes its replacement.

Anger/rage and grief/pain
This is when after facing the reality of your loss, you become angry. The anger could be directed at the person or animal who has left you (such as 'how dare you leave me like this!') or anger towards a higher being (whether that is God, angels, the universe, or some other deity you may believe in), or even 'why not someone else?'. It could also be the grief and pain of knowing that you won't be able to share things with that person or pet again, go on those walks, have those all-night talks, or feel that kind of love again.

Bargaining
As you manage to express your feelings of anger without feeling shame or guilt, you enter the bargaining stage. This is where you try to bargain with God (or whoever you believe in) or try to make some other kind of deal — for example, 'if you spare me/him/her their life, I promise I'll always go to church'. Or, in the case of the dying patients with Dr Kubler-Ross, it could be bargaining for something else such as 'please don't let me die until my child gets married'. For the person already in the grief cycle, bargaining may come in the way of asking your loved one to come back in return for you doing something.

Depression

The next stage leads to a feeling of depression. A dying patient faces the realisation that nothing they do is going to change the reality of what is happening to them. For those who lose someone or something, there is a feeling of intense sadness and pain as they wonder how on earth they will ever make it through. There is no bright side to this stage and nothing that can be said that will seemingly make any difference.

Acceptance

After time progressing through the stages, there comes a final acceptance. This stage does not mean the person is happy, but they are no longer feeling angry or depressed. In the ACT approach this stage would be described as accepting the reality of what is.

While grief is generally a very unpleasant thing to experience, it can often help to bring people together. Sometimes it is a reality check on our own mortality and a reminder to 'live for the moment' in the here and now and be mindful rather than worry about the past or future.

I should point out that there is no 'set' timeframe for how long you should grieve. There are no rules or guidelines for time spent in grief for a partner, a pet, a family member, or old school friend etc. It takes as long as it takes. However, I would add that you should expect to see some improvement in your mood as time progresses. If you are still feeling the same level of grief some months or even years after the initial loss, then it may be time to speak to a professional to make sure it is not turning into complicated grief.

One thing I also noticed with my own clients going through the grief process is that they did not want to laugh or be happy. Many felt that it would be perceived as being inconsiderate, disrespectful, or even rude to act happy when someone has just lost their life. But I will mention this — would your loved one want you to be sad and miserable every single day? When you are able to start improving your mood, be it having a little laugh at something or thinking about something other than the person/animal who has passed, it can indicate your recovery throughout this process. It can signal that you are starting to move through the grief and is also a reminder that you still have your life to live — as hard as that may seem sometimes.

Some of the things that I recommend to my clients going through a grief process is to have a dedicated 'worry' or 'crying' time each day. So rather than crying all day and night, set aside a dedicated time to cry. As you go through the day and feel ready to cry at the drop of a hat, remind yourself that you'll allow yourself to cry at 3 pm (or whatever time you dedicate). This way you are still acknowledging your grief but are not being all-consumed by it. It does not mean you don't care or respect your loved one — it means that you are trying to work your way through the grief as best you can.

Another recommended thing to do while grieving is to write a journal. Write about how you are feeling, what you are feeling, your loved one, or the special things you used to do. Being able to express it healthily can be very comforting.

And for those of you who are spiritually minded like me, you may like to talk (out loud or in your mind) to your loved one as if they are still there. You know they cannot answer as they used to or return from death, but if you find comfort from feeling their presence and being a part of your life, then this very personal experience is yours to have. As I often say, no one can prove the existence of an afterlife or not, so if it helps you to believe you are still connecting with your passed-over loved one, then so be it. As one of my favourite sayings by Stuart Chase goes, 'For those who don't believe, no proof is possible. For those who do believe, no proof is necessary'.

Chapter 10

Coping with Change and Adversity

Life can sometimes feel out of control. It can change in the blink of an eye and often feels like it goes by in a snap. If we are not mindful, we can miss a lot of the good things that are happening.

If I think back to 2020 when the COVID pandemic made its entrance into the world, one thing that stands out for me is how quickly people had to adapt. There were lockdowns, businesses closing, students being forced to undertake online learning, people working from home, veterinary clinics working kerbside, job losses, mental health issues, restrictions on travel, families and friends not being able to see each other in person, and a whole lot of fear.

Unfortunately, these kinds of situations are outside of our control, but we can control how we respond to them and how we choose to behave. For example, I might not have been able to control whether I could go to the gym, but I could control whether I continued to exercise at or around my home and look after my health by eating nutritionally and taking the appropriate supplements to try and keep myself as healthy as possible.

Regardless of what life throws at you, unless you are totally incapacitated, I believe we still have the choice to decide how we want to respond. As I say, whether you accept the situation or not, the reality of it doesn't change.

I want to share with you some of my tips and suggestions for coping with change and adversity. Some of them you may already be familiar with, but hopefully there are a few little gems there that you can add to your toolbox.

First of all, though, I have a few self-check questions for you. The more of these you answer 'yes' to, the more it could indicate a higher level of risk. Please don't use this as a self-diagnosis. Rather, it is designed to alert you to some of the factors that could indicate you may not be coping as well as expected. If you do find yourself answering 'yes' to all the questions, then I would encourage you to seek out some professional support to work through these and help you to address them in a healthy and safe way.

Self-check — are you at risk?

Mood changes
Have you noticed any changes to your mood, such as becoming more irritable, more emotional than usual, or feeling angrier with no apparent reason or in a way that is uncharacteristic for you?

Insomnia or sleep disturbances
Are you struggling to get to sleep or stay asleep, waking earlier than normal and not being able to get back to

sleep, or having other disturbances to your sleep (in the absence of weather conditions, noisy neighbours, barking dogs, etc.) such as disturbing or repetitive dreams?

Consuming more (or starting) alcohol or other substances
Have you started drinking or consuming more alcohol or other substances than normal or begun consuming these for the first time? By other substances, I'm not just referring to illegal drugs, it could also be a reliance on over-the-counter supplements or herbal remedies that you can't do without.

Appetite changes
Are you feeling less hungry than normal, or perhaps you feel so ravenous you could eat everything in sight? Or do you fluctuate between the two?

Racing mind
Is your mind racing? Are your thoughts constantly chatting away in your head and making it hard to concentrate?

Catastrophic or ruminating thoughts
What are your thoughts telling you? Are they positive, helpful, and calming thoughts, or are they more negative and unhelpful? Often, we get caught up in thoughts about the past and ruminate about them, which can sometimes lead to depression. Other times we may buy into thoughts about the future and start catastrophising about them, which can lead to anxiety.

Behavioural changes
Are you acting differently from what is 'normal' for you, such as arriving late to work, being rude to people, or

having a nonchalant attitude towards people and things? Maybe you have stopped showering or taking pride in your appearance, or your favourite new activity is to slump in front of a screen endlessly eating junk food, whereas normally you wouldn't dream of doing this?

The self-check points above are not an exhaustive list of all the indicators that could signal you may not be coping so well with change or adversity, but they are a good starting point for some of the things I would normally ask a client and begin to investigate further if I were concerned about their wellbeing.

Are there any other things you have noticed yourself doing that are uncharacteristic of you? If so, it might be time to seek some professional support to nip it in the bud before it gets harder to manage.

As well as practising the resiliency tips I've shared in this book, there are a few other things you can do to try and enhance and/or maintain your wellbeing. I've broken down the wellbeing tips here into personal and work. While I think this should be self-explanatory, these personal tips are generally suggested for your personal life, and the work tips are for your professional life. Just as it's important to look after ourselves outside of work, we need to make sure we have a healthy work/life balance. Therefore, it is equally as important to practice wellbeing and self-care in our professional lives too.

Wellbeing Tips — Personal

- reduce your time on social media and try not to watch the same unnecessary things

- set and maintain a routine to keep some structure in your day-to-day activities
- practice relaxation activities that are safe, healthy, and legal
- keep a gratitude diary and write down all the things you are grateful for each day
- at the end of each day, write down three good things about yourself, something you have seen or heard, or something you have done
- practice random acts of kindness
- learn and apply evidence-based coping strategies (such as ACT)
- stay informed about the news via reliable sources only, but don't become bogged down in fear-mongering or negative information
- keep in touch with family and friends digitally if you can't do so in-person
- spring clean the house
- research or study something you're personally interested in
- continue with or take up new hobbies
- watch or listen to something funny
- listen to your favourite health and wellbeing podcasts
- recognise what is and isn't within your control
- set SMART goals for your personal life
- do some gardening
- exercise
- take a nap or sleep in if it's appropriate to do so

- read a book
- stream a favourite TV series and watch a couple of episodes at a time
- enjoy some colouring in
- play cards or board games.

Wellbeing Tips — Work

- listen to your favourite business podcasts
- set SMART career or business goals
- catch up on your professional development
- research or study something you're professionally interested in
- prepare blogs for the business/organisation's website
- create e-newsletters for your client database
- declutter your work environment
- help a colleague (aka random act of kindness!)
- create work social media posts
- organise a team-building day, lunch, or event
- utilise workplace employee assistance programs (EAP/EWP) if needed
- practice the three good things exercise with your colleagues
- keep a gratitude jar with your colleagues and take turns reading them out
- give a colleague or client a compliment (make sure it's appropriate though!)

- encourage your colleagues to engage in wellbeing activities
- set up a workplace wellbeing program.

As I hope you are beginning to realise now but will repeat to make sure it is starting to be absorbed:

- don't be afraid to put yourself first — if you don't, who will?
- self-care is not selfish — it is essential
- speak up and set boundaries
- if you mean no, then say no (which means don't say yes if you mean no!)
- stop worrying about what others will think if you don't agree with them or do things their way
- opinions are like heads — everyone has one, but your opinion should be the most important to you.

Chapter 11

Compassion Fatigue

There can be some confusion between compassion fatigue, imposter syndrome, and burnout. Some people misdiagnose themselves with imposter syndrome when they are really experiencing compassion fatigue. Others think they are experiencing compassion fatigue when it's burnout. And still others may never have heard any of these terms and have no idea what I'm talking about here! Let's look at compassion fatigue in a little more detail first.

Compassion fatigue is common in the helping and healing professions and can be defined as a state of preoccupation and tension where the suffering of those being helped can extend to secondary traumatic stress for the helper. It is a state experienced by those helping distressed animals or humans. When the helper or healer is trying to remain compassionate to both the other person or animal, this can result in a difficulty to effectively maintain a healthy balance of their own emotions and feelings, particularly in times of trauma or end-of-life situations.

Imagine you have been at work for 12 hours and on your feet much of that time. Then imagine you must come home, cook dinner, feed the pets, bath the children, make lunches for the next day, put a load of washing on, empty the dishwasher, and read an article you promised your friend you would read. Now picture someone asking if you could go and join them for a workout in the gym at the end of all this. Do you feel exhausted just at the thought of it? Visualise doing this every day and try to get a sense of how fatiguing it would become, possibly very quickly. While this level of fatigue is more of a physical nature, compassion fatigue is where you feel that same sense of fatigue and exhaustion, but it is from experiencing a high level of constant compassionate emotion rather than physical exertion.

Compassion fatigue can take weeks or even years to surface and can occur when there is an overwhelming level of concern or care for others, but over time the ability to feel compassionate towards others reduces through overuse.

Symptoms to look out for

Compassion fatigue can have many negative and unhelpful effects on wellbeing, such as (but not limited to):

Insomnia
You may struggle to get to sleep or stay asleep, waking earlier than normal and not being able to get back to sleep. You may be having other disturbances to your sleep (in the absence of weather conditions, noisy neighbours, barking dogs, etc.), such as disturbing or repetitive dreams.

Depression
I have covered depression in a bit more depth in a previous chapter, so please go back and refresh yourself on the signs and symptoms if need be, but just to recap, some of the signs include:

- loss of interest in tasks and routines
- changes in sleeping patterns
- irritability, fatigue, and agitation
- hopelessness
- worrying (ruminating) and negative thinking
- suicidal ideation.

Absenteeism from work or social events
While absenteeism from work can be due to a few reasons (including workplace conflict), it can also be an indicator of compassion fatigue. When you are so fatigued with being at work and the pressures of enduring the need to be compassionate, the thought of going back in there again for what may feel like 'Groundhog Day' can be overwhelming — hence some people elect to take some time off from work.

*Decline in cognitive function,
not being able to focus or concentrate*
When you are so focused and consumed with your thoughts and feeling exhausted from fatigue, the mind can't cope as well as it normally would. The thoughts can be all-consuming, and it can feel like you are trying to find a place for a book on a bookshelf that is already stacked full. There is nowhere for that book to go, nor can the existing books on the shelf be easily removed if they are so

crammed full of other books. Just like our mind — when it is overwhelmed and crammed full of thoughts, it is as if there is no room left to process all the different things running through it.

Feeling a lack of self-worth, hope, meaning, and morale
Experiencing any kind of fatigue can leave you feeling a lack of motivation. You have no real desire to do much more than sit and rest. Compassion fatigue is just like this. It can leave you feeling so emotionally drained that you have no room left to process other thoughts or feelings, including your sense of self-worth, your optimism, your meaning and purpose, and your morale.

Increase in emotional symptoms such as anger, crying, or outbursts
As I mentioned above, when we are overwhelmed with compassion fatigue, it can feel all-consuming. We don't have any room left in our minds to think rationally about things, and this leaves us feeling exasperated and on edge. We have little 'left in the tank' to cope with things. In this state our emotions are prone to metaphorically 'explode' and present themselves as anger, crying, or other outbursts.

Impairments in judgement and behaviour
This is similar to the earlier listed decline in cognitive function. Our mind is so full and preoccupied with other thoughts that we don't have the scope to be able to handle our thoughts clearly and logically when required. This affects our decision-making ability and our sense of judgement about our behaviours.

Becoming isolated from others
As with absenteeism, withdrawing from other people or situations can be a way of removing ourselves from the stress that threatens to overwhelm us. We tend to isolate ourselves from others, so we don't have to take on board any of their issues or emotions, as well as not having anyone question us or put pressure on us. Likewise, we can isolate ourselves as a way of avoidance. We should be mindful though that sometimes getting away from others allows us to take time out for self-care.

Feelings of anger towards other people or events
Ever heard the expression 'the grass is always greener on the other side'? We can feel anger towards other people or events for a number of reasons. Sometimes it may be because we perceive them as being responsible for our own circumstances; other times it could be because we resent them for their seemingly 'perfect' life without any issues. It is good to stop and try to think clearly about where our anger comes from. Are we just upset because over there is something that looks like a greener pasture?

Are you at risk?

As with some of the other self-checks in this book, the points below are not about forming a diagnosis but rather an indicator for further exploration. The more of these that can be related to your own experience, the higher the possibility that they represent compassion fatigue. Please seek out support from a qualified mental health professional if you feel you may be experiencing compassion fatigue. Some signs of compassion fatigue include:

- losing of compassion towards some people, but an increase towards others

- feeling regularly disgusted or bored, particularly in the workplace
- struggling to get to work each day
- regularly waking up feeling tired
- experiencing aches and/or pains
- experiencing illness
- feeling irritated and frustrated more easily than normal
- feeling like you are putting more effort into your work but not achieving as much
- feeling that some things at work that used to feel 'normal' now feel traumatic
- feeling that you are just not functioning effectively in life.

Compassion fatigue can lead to other issues, such as anxiety, depression, and burnout, if not treated effectively. Continually exposing yourself to the same difficult situations, again and again, is unlikely to leave you feeling fantastic — nor is it likely to improve unless you address it in a healthy way.

You may like to try some of the coping strategies mentioned in this book, but please always be sure to reach out to a qualified mental health professional for a correct diagnosis and appropriate support.

Chapter 12

Burnout

I often find that the term burnout gets thrown around very easily, but people don't always know the true meaning of what it really is. As I mentioned in the chapter on compassion fatigue, there can be some confusion between burnout, compassion fatigue, and imposter syndrome, so I want to delve a little deeper into this now.

What is Burnout?

Burnout is not related to trauma per se but is a process that gradually cumulates over a period of time due to things like workplace stress, an increased workload, or other work-related pressures. Sometimes doing the same thing day-in, day-out can lead to burnout.

Generally marked by withdrawal and emotional exhaustion, burnout is often referred to as being or feeling 'worn out' and can affect anyone in any profession. It isn't always present in people who suffer compassion fatigue (and vice versa) — that is, the two are mutually exclusive. However, they can also co-exist together in some cases.

For the person experiencing burnout, sadly, things that once created a drive, passion, or sense of enthusiasm are replaced by negative, cynical, unhelpful, and unpleasant thoughts.

I'm not ashamed to say I have experienced burnout twice in my professional career. The first time I was a reasonably new graduate psychologist. I was counselling a client, listening to them explain the difficulties they were facing in their life, when suddenly the thought popped into my head: 'I don't really care about your problems'. That was when I knew I needed to take some proactive measures. I ended up leaving that job and started teaching at a College — I dare say I also experienced some compassion fatigue with that burnout as well due to the amount of secondary trauma (aka vicarious trauma) I was exposed to from listening to my clients day after day.

The second time was quite a few years later, after finishing my doctoral degree and working in a senior position in academia. The workload was intense — too much for one person, and in my opinion (and that of many of my colleagues experiencing similar things), completely unrealistic. I had no compassion fatigue in that role, and while I loved my job and the team I managed and worked with, the demands of the workload were too much. Fortunately, I recognised the symptoms early on and spoke to my boss. I elected not to renew my contract, and as expected, the symptoms went away.

Stages of Burnout

The stages leading to burnout can be recognised and defined as:

- enthusiasm
- stagnation
- frustration
- apathy.

Enthusiasm
Think about a time when you were starting a new job you were really looking forward to. You went to work each day and were enthusiastic about it, absorbing everything like a sponge and looking forward to going in the next day. Maybe you even happily worked some overtime because you enjoyed it so much. You were enthusiastic about special projects or contributing your ideas and had it all planned out how you'd make a positive difference in the workplace.

Stagnation
After a little while though, it's like the novelty wears off. The enthusiasm and motivation you initially felt have dwindled, and now it's just 'so-so'. Some days may even feel fairly ordinary, and you start making sure you finish at the end of your shift without putting in any extra time or effort. In this stage you're just 'going with the flow'.

Frustration
After the stagnation comes frustration. Things (or even people) you used to enjoy working with now annoy you. You find yourself getting frustrated at the slightest thing, and you might even notice yourself complaining to your co-workers and starting to feel quite cynical about the workplace.

Apathy
Oh dear! Now you have progressed through to the final stage into burnout — apathy. This is where you feel void of all emotions, interests, feelings, or even concerns about the workplace. In this stage, you feel as if you are 'done' and can't possibly go to work another day. The thought of it might even make you feel sick (I know it did for me!).

What are the symptoms?
Some of the symptoms of burnout may be like that of compassion fatigue and some other psychological conditions, and commonly include:

- nausea
- feelings of stress
- insomnia
- anxiety
- absenteeism
- withdrawal / lack of interest, passion, motivation, and drive
- dread at the thought of having to go to work
- frustration and/or anger
- exhaustion and fatigue
- responding in a negative way to others
- appearing more cynical
- inability to function effectively (focus, concentration).

Commonalities with compassion fatigue
As I mentioned earlier, there can be some confusion between compassion fatigue and burnout, particularly as

some of the symptoms are similar. These are some of the things the two have in common:

- there may be physical, mental, and emotional exhaustion
- the individual may experience a reduction in their sense of meaning and accomplishment in their work
- they may tend to isolate themselves from others and interact less
- they may also disconnect or depersonalise themselves from things.

So how do you know if you are experiencing compassion fatigue, burnout, or both? Well, it can be a bit tricky depending on the range of symptoms you have, but I would encourage you to seek help from a qualified mental health professional and have them help you to correctly identify what may be going on for you. But in the meantime, here are a couple of things to note. Burnout tends to emerge over a period of time (a bit like the expression 'the body whispers before it shouts', whereas compassion fatigue is more likely to have a rapid onset. Generally, there is a faster recovery from compassion fatigue if it is identified and dealt with effectively in the early stages, whereas burnout can take quite a bit longer to recover from.

What can you do?

There are several things you can do to help someone (or yourself) experiencing compassion fatigue and/or burnout:

- help them to find someone they can talk to (a psychologist or other qualified mental health professional can be a great place to start)

- encourage them to adopt good eating and exercise routines
- take time off if need be
- try to get enough quality sleep
- discourage the use of alcohol or drugs as a way of self-medicating
- encourage them to develop interest and engage in hobbies and activities outside of work
- ensure they adopt excellent self-care
- help them to set boundaries
- maintain open lines of communication about their feelings with their social support network
- try to make them feel comfortable and safe by speaking up and reaching out for support.

What not to do

Just as there are things you can do to help, there are also some things you should not encourage they do — such as:

- try and place the blame on other people
- spend excessively on material things
- start complaining to other colleagues and dragging them into the negativity and resentment
- self-medicate
- have an affair (you don't need the added stress of a relationship issue on top of the burnout!)
- work longer and/or harder
- keep quiet and suffer in silence
- neglect your own interests and needs.

In summary

Burnout can be treated, but it may take time. One of my mottos is that it is best to be proactive rather than reactive. Seek out professional support early to give yourself the best possible chance of a correct diagnosis and beneficial treatment. You can't treat what you don't acknowledge.

Learn how to recognise your symptoms and how to differentiate between compassion fatigue and burnout so you can identify them sooner rather than later. It can be helpful to practice mindfulness regularly so you can identify symptoms early and take a proactive approach (refer to the strategies in ACT if you need a refresher). It is also important not to judge or criticise other people who may be experiencing compassion fatigue or burnout — most of us are doing the best we can with what we have, and remember, no one is so perfect that they are better than anyone else.

And it goes without saying — reach out for support if you need to.

Chapter 13

Dealing with Imposter Syndrome

Ever feel like you are a phony in the workplace and not really qualified to be there, even though you are?

Before we get into this chapter, let me ask you a few questions...

- If you are completely honest with yourself, do you believe your failings are all your own fault, but your successes are pure good luck or a fluke?
- Are you forever wondering when the 'fraud police' are going to come and expose you for being a phony?
- Would you believe me if I told you that you weren't alone?

So how did you go answering these questions? Did you answer 'yes' to all or most of them? Read on.

What is Imposter Syndrome?

If you have ever felt like you didn't belong somewhere or that your colleagues, friends, and associates are going to discover you are a phony and a fraud and that you really don't deserve success, then you are not alone. These feelings are referred to as 'imposter phenomenon' or 'imposter syndrome', and they affect a wide range of people from all aspects of life.

If you can relate to any of the following statements, you may have imposter syndrome:
- I feel like I'm a fake and a phony.
- I feel like I'm a fraud, and I don't belong here.
- I'm inadequate and really don't have what it takes.
- I have no idea what I'm doing – and people are going to find out.
- I'm not like the rest of my colleagues.
- Whatever gave me the idea that I'm smart and/or experienced enough?
- I don't deserve this success.

The term 'imposter syndrome' was originally coined by two psychologists to describe women who did not feel as though they were successful, even though they were. These women felt their success had nothing to do with their efforts or abilities but put it down to things like 'good luck' or a 'fluke'.

With imposter syndrome, there is a fear of self-doubt that everyone will find out you are a phony when 'the truth comes out'. Those experiencing this syndrome think they are the only person who is feeling this way, yet the reality is that we all feel insecure at some point, but some people are more conscious of it than others. While it was originally referred to as a term that affected women, it is now known that men, too, experience this phenomenon.

And research suggests that up to 70% of people will experience these feelings!

What causes imposter syndrome?

As with many psychological conditions and issues, there is never really just one particular cause. Sometimes we don't even know what causes some of the things people go through as there can be so many contributing factors. However, with imposter syndrome, it is believed the following factors play a contributing role:

- personality traits such as anxiety or neuroticism (perfectionists may be susceptible)
- family factors such as parenting styles
- facing new settings or environments, such as starting a new role at work.

What are the symptoms?

The following factors have been distinguished as contributing to the syndrome. At least two of these are required to be present for the experience of 'impostorism' to be considered:

- the need to be special or the best
- trying to emulate a superhero through extreme effort
- a fear of failure
- denial of one's ability
- discounting praise
- feeling fear and guilt about success.

There are different ways people will experience imposter syndrome, but some common examples include:
- overworking
- undermining yourself
- fearing failure
- perfectionism
- discounting praise.

What can you do about it?

One of the ways to try and combat imposter syndrome is to acknowledge the thoughts and feelings (I'd suggest using ACT or CBT for this) and put them into perspective by gathering evidence and extracting the self-doubt — such as:
- Ask yourself, is there any evidence to prove you are a failure?
- Ask yourself, is it helpful to have these thoughts that you are a phony?
- Ask yourself if these thoughts and feelings are realistic?
- Ask yourself whether buying into these thoughts and feelings (and acting as if they were true) will help you in the long run?
- Ask yourself if these thoughts and feelings are aligned with your values?
- Remind yourself that the only difference between yourself and someone else who does not experience imposter syndrome is how they respond to challenges

- Learn how to value constructive criticism and feedback rather than seeing it as something negative that you need to be defensive about
- Think about how you could be slowing things down for your team if you don't have the answer, and avoid asking for help
- Share what you are feeling and experiencing with trusted family, friends, mentors, or a qualified mental health professional
- Know that what you are feeling is experienced by other people (remember that 70% estimate?) and can be quite normal
- Consider speaking to a psychologist or other qualified mental health professional to gather strategies on how to work through your feelings in a safe way
- Don't let your thoughts of doubt control your actions.

What else can you do?

Some quick and easy things you can also try are:

- strike a power pose for two minutes (picture 'Wonder Woman' with her hands on her hips)
- give up on the need to be perfect
- be mindful and check in with yourself and how you are thinking and feeling
- own your successes rather than discrediting them
- don't compare yourself to others — there's only one of them, and one of you. You can't be anyone else, so own who you are and be the best you can be

- practice gratitude, 'three good things', and accept praise
- have a cheer squad.

In Summary

By now you should realise the focus of this book is on self-care and wellbeing, so it should come as no surprise that I suggest you look after yourself.

Practicing mindfulness regularly (even setting an alarm or having a reminder system) so it becomes an automatic process can be helpful. That way, you can check in on how you are thinking and feeling and nip anything negative in the bud before it escalates to catastrophising or rumination or imposterism.

Thoughts become things, so make sure you are not 'buying into' and believing every thought that comes into your head. Just because you are thinking it, it doesn't mean it is true!

And lastly, remind yourself that you are human — there is no such thing as 'perfect' so please do not place these unrealistic expectations on yourself. Don't forget that most of us will experience imposter syndrome at some stage.

Chapter 14

Coping Strategies

As I often say to people, I firmly believe that no matter what is going on in our lives (be it personal or work-related), we still need to be able to cope with what is going on. But sometimes this seems easier said than done, right?

Here's an interesting fact. It only takes 600 milliseconds for the thinking part of our brain (the frontal cortex) to register an emotion to something, but just 100 milliseconds for our brain to react to it. This can explain why sometimes the emotion on someone's face already shows how they feel about something before they can verbalise it! Ever notice someone's face when they receive a gift they don't like, but tell everyone how wonderful it is? Yep — by the time you decide how you want to react, your face has already shown that emotion for 500 milliseconds!

This leads nicely into the behaviour chain — what we believe is going on whenever we think about what leads to a behaviour. Typically, there is a trigger (something that triggers a response in you — so it could be a person who reminds you of a treasured friend or someone yelling at you which triggers a response), which then leads to our thoughts or beliefs about what this trigger means to us. This can then lead to how this makes us feel emotionally (such as happy, sad, angry, or depressed), which then results in the action or behaviour we take to respond to the trigger — which then ends in the consequences of those actions (be it good, bad, or indifferent). So, the behaviour chain looks something like this:

Trigger ⇢ thought ⇢ emotions ⇢ action ⇢ consequences

The key is to be mindful enough to notice your thoughts and emotions once the trigger is activated and choose more helpful and healthy responses to that trigger. This is what ACT teaches us to do.

Being able to regulate your emotions and have good emotional regulation is important. Using strategies such as speaking in emotions may be helpful — for example, 'when X happens, I feel Y'. Noticing your primary and secondary emotions is also important. The emotions you feel as soon as you encounter a trigger are your primary emotions. The emotions you feel after these primary emotions are known as your secondary emotions. They are triggered by your primary emotions and not the trigger itself. Think of your secondary emotions as the reactions you have emotionally to your primary emotions. To give you a few examples:

- When you are yelled at, you might feel angry (primary), then you might feel sad (secondary) because you feel you deserved to be yelled at and had no right to object.
- When you pass an exam, you might feel ecstatic (primary), then you might feel anxious (secondary)

because you shouldn't feel too confident as you missed some answers.
- When you hear a crash in the night, you might feel scared (primary) then you might feel shame at feeling scared at nothing (secondary).

Exposure is also a good way to learn better coping. When you expose yourself to a difficult situation over and over, it can become easier until it becomes a habit. When you continue to expose yourself to the same stressful things, you may experience stress or anxiety but generally each time you expose yourself to it the intensity reduces — and the more resilient you may become.

The flip side of this is to remember not to practise too much avoidance. If you continually avoid a situation that is uncomfortable, you will start to build a habit of avoidance. It is important to remember that avoiding something doesn't change the reality of it. For example, if you are avoiding thinking about the work meeting you have on Monday, or how you are going to afford to pay next week's rent payment, avoidance won't change the reality that you have a work meeting on Monday or still need to find a way to pay next week's rent.

When we think of anxiety, we generally perceive there is something to be fearful of. There are a few acronyms for FEAR which I quite like:

- False Evidence Appearing Real
- Forget Everything and Run (avoidance)
- Face Everything and Rise (exposure).

You can also think of your responses in two ways — the behavioural response and subjective experience. The behavioural response is the external experience (or consequence of your actions), whereas the subjective experience is what you feel internally, such as the physiological consequences.

All behaviours, though are a form of communication — it's just that some may be better ways of communicating than others. There are four main ways of communicating:

- Passive communication — this is where the person does not express their opinions, beliefs, needs, or thoughts. It is like they are taking a passive approach and acting as if it does not matter.
- Passive-aggressive communication — the person's actions may be passive but have an aggressive undertone to it — such as gesturing behind someone's back or muttering comments under their breath.
- Aggressive communication — usually loud, demanding, or intimidating. The aggressive person wants to be heard no matter what.
- Assertive communication — the ideal way to communicate. This is where you get your message across in a way that is respectful to yourself and the other person/s, making 'I' statements rather than accusatory 'you' statements.

It is important to make a general note here that there is a difference between *distraction* and *avoidance*. Distraction is a temporary way of removing yourself from something that might be intense or unhelpful so you can step back into it after you've had time to withdraw from it and see things with a clear mind. Avoidance is when you don't want to acknowledge something and do whatever it takes to stop it from returning.

Psychological Flexibility

This is what ACT is based on. It is one of the main determinants of emotional, psychological, and mental health. It essentially is about how you can change your cognitions and what is going on internally (such as attitudes, thoughts, and behaviours) in order to thrive in the outside world (with the environment, other people, or different situations). It is about being flexible psychologically, no matter what is going on. Essentially, it's like weathering life's ups-downs-and in-betweens.

Dealing with change is tough. Have you ever noticed how your mind often knows deep-down which choice you should make, but you don't always listen to it and end up acting in some less-than-desirable way? Focus on the things you can control rather than those you can't, such as what you eat, how and when you exercise, how you speak to yourself, and things like breathing for relaxation.

Metacognition is a psychological term that describes an understanding and awareness of a person's thought processes and thoughts. You can think of this as 'thoughts about thoughts, cognition about cognition, and knowing about knowing'.

Overgeneralisation is a term used to describe taking one small piece of information but then using it to form a huge picture. I think most of us have done this at some stage. It could be helpful to reframe these thought distortions into something more positive to try to combat this in a healthy way. For example, rather than thinking, 'I'm such a loser because of XYZ' acknowledge the thought, but then replace it with something more positive such as 'even though I didn't enjoy XYZ I have now learnt that I am able to do ABC instead'. Or even something simple like replacing 'I've failed' with 'I've learned'.

It's also important to remember that your imagination can also get out of control, particularly when it is focused on the worst-case scenario (I'm sure we've all been there and done that!). When you feel yourself getting caught up in all the 'what ifs' recognise these can just be thought distortions and are not necessarily true or going to happen. Use your imagination (or strategies from ACT) to think about the likelihood that your worst-case scenario would realistically happen — with an understanding that your thought distortions may be very far-fetched.

Creative visualisation can be helpful if used correctly — visualise the best-case scenarios and not the worst-case scenarios. Visualisation can sometimes be beneficial when conquering triggers or fears, such as imagining you are holding a snake (if you have a fear of snakes) and slowly stroking it and feeling how soft its skin is.

If you feel like you are about to 'buy into' triggers and the consequences won't be helpful, you might like to try the D.E.A.D.S exercise from *Noom.com* (and just to be clear, I'm not talking about dying here — rather the following acronym):

- D elay (delay your response for 10–30 minutes as around 90% of urges pass within this time)
- E scape (remove yourself from the situation or environment so the reminder isn't there)
- A ccept (as we teach in ACT — accept the reality of what-is but let it pass)

D ispute (dispute the situation by asking yourself if this is a thought distortion)

S ubstitute (whatever it is that is unhealthy or unhelpful with something that is more healthy or helpful).

Remember, every setback is an opportunity to learn!

I have presented many webinars and workshops over the years on how to use ACT, and it is generally one of the go-to strategies I use with my clients. It's also a strategy I use myself. (Just because I'm a psychologist it doesn't mean I don't have unhelpful thoughts and feelings like other people do. It just means that I am probably better equipped than many people to be able to deal with it!)

While I covered ACT in my book *Coping with Stress and Burnout as a Veterinarian*, I appreciate that many of you reading this book would not yet have had the opportunity to read it, so I wanted to provide a brief overview here.

What is ACT?

ACT aims to help people move forward in a way that is in line with their values. Values are those things you want to stand for, the things that give you meaning and purpose. Essentially ACT is about accepting the things you can't change or control and committing to take action (behave) in line with your values.

There are six core processes used in ACT with the overall aim of psychological flexibility. These six processes are detailed below.

Mindfulness (being present). This stage is about being in the present moment, or the 'here and now'. When you are being present, it allows you to experience what is going on in that moment rather than those thoughts and feelings controlling your behaviour by responding on autopilot.

Acceptance. The stage of acceptance is considered the 'open up' stage. Acceptance means you can allow and make room for emotions that may be painful, or sensations, urges, or feelings — without struggling to try and change their form or frequency.

Cognitive defusion. Often referred to just as 'defusion', it is considered the 'watch your thoughts' step. This step is about being able to detach yourself from those memories, thoughts, feelings, and images, and separating yourself from them.

Self as context. This stage of ACT can be described as the stage of 'pure awareness'. It can be a little difficult to understand, as it refers to what is described as two elements of the mind that are quite distinct — the 'observing self' and the 'thinking self'.

Committed action. This stage is the final process in ACT and can be considered the 'do what it takes' stage. It is important to note that just because you live in line with your values, it does not always mean you will avoid unpleasant situations, which is unrealistic. You need to act on your values to get results — merely just thinking about them will not make the process work.

Values. As mentioned earlier, your values are the things you want to stand for — those things that give you your sense of meaning and purpose. Values are also actions.

ACT in Action

Step 1 – Mindfulness

The first step is to get into a state of mindfulness. While these aren't the only mindfulness strategies, they can be a good starting point for those of you who aren't familiar with mindfulness and don't know where to start. You do not need to do each one of these — just pick one that resonates with you:

- name five things you can see, five things you can hear, and five things that have contact with your body now
- notice your thoughts on a leaf, conveyor belt, or across the tv
- describe in as much detail as you can something in the room
- become mindful of your breathing.

Step 2 – Example questions to ask yourself
Once you are in a state of mindfulness and in the present moment, bring your attention now to your thoughts and feelings. Then ask yourself:

- Is this a helpful thought/feeling?
- If I act on these thoughts/feelings does it help me to take action to create the life that I want?
- What would I get from buying into this thought/feeling?
- Does this thought/feeling help me in the long run?

If your answer to the above questions are 'no' then proceed to the next step. If the answer is 'yes', then it would indicate the thought/feeling is not bothering you and therefore it is not necessary to proceed to step three.

Step 3 – Example defusion statements
The aim of cognitive defusion is to get the thought/feeling out of your head/body to a place where you can see it for what it really is — just a thought (i.e., bunch of words your mind is telling you) or feeling. In this step just notice the thought/feeling and do any of the following:

- either silently or out loud, say 'thank you mind for the thought that...'
- either silently or out loud say 'I'm having the thought that...'
- sing the thought to the tune of a song or say it in a silly voice
- repeat the thought and speed it up or slow it down.

Step 4 – Values
In this final step this is where you take action (i.e., how you respond or behave) in line with your values. Think about your values in the following core areas, and then choose how you would like to respond, using these values.

- work/education
- personal growth/health
- leisure
- relationships.

For example, suppose you value being professional at work and providing excellent customer service. In that case, yelling at a rude customer and telling them they are horrible is probably not consistent with your values of professionalism and customer service!

Despite the thought that you might want to yell at the customer and say something mean, what would be the long-term consequence of doing so? Would you be happy with that consequence? Would that contribute to your state of wellbeing? I'm guessing the answer to this is 'no' (as this action goes *against* your values), so you are likely to end up feeling bad in the long run if you acted on those thoughts. Instead, think about how you could respond in a professional, customer-service-focused way (while you *just notice* the thoughts or feelings telling you otherwise) and then act in line with these values. Generally speaking, in the long run you will likely be glad you did act this way, rather than being rude and unprofessional.

I often recommend we have a 'toolbox' of resources, and while my preference is to use ACT as my go-to coping strategy, I do believe it's important to have a few other strategies to call upon when they are needed.

Problem Solving

When you are faced with a problem, it can feel like you have a mountain to cross, and often you feel like you can't see the wood for the trees. However, a strategy one of my fellow psychologists, Dr Peter Stebbins, taught me when faced with a problem that you have some control over (such as speaking up to someone after they were rude to you) was this — use a problem-solving approach. Think about all the options available to you, consider the potential consequences of each of these options, and then proceed with the one you feel will be the best. Have a look at the following example.

You are at work and your co-worker Judy makes a snide remark about something you did earlier that day. You may not have spoken up at the time (which could be a passive approach — or it could be that you are considering your options by stepping back and not reacting straight away), but it is really bugging you now. So, you think about what you can do:

1. You could just ignore it and hope it goes away — but the consequence of this action could be that instead of going away, the resentment starts to build inside of you.
2. You could complain to another co-worker about how rude Judy was to you — but the consequence of this action may be that what you say gets repeated to Judy, potentially opening the door for more conflict.
3. You could choose to be assertive and speak to Judy and tell her honestly how her remark made you feel and that you would appreciate it if she could please be more respectful to you in future. The consequence of this action may be that Judy laughs off your comment, but you will have taken the opportunity to be assertive and stand up for yourself in a respectful way. Or it could be that Judy apologises and tells you she didn't mean anything hurtful by her remarks.
4. You could use evidence-based coping skills with ACT or some other helpful strategy.

Which of these will make you feel better in the long run? The aim is to choose the one you think will give you the best results and then act on it. If you don't get the expected result, reconsider your options, and go through the process again.

Emotion-focused coping

If the problem is outside of your control though, you could use emotion-focused coping — strategies such as ACT or CBT. Here's an example. You really want to get your lawn mown and a new herb garden planted on the weekend, but it's predicted to rain. It's the only weekend you've had available in a long time, and it could be a few weekends before you have the opportunity again. You might be feeling quite anxious about whether or not you will be able to get the gardening done, yet the outcome is outside of your control. What do you do to cope with your distress?

Cognitive Behavioural Therapy

Cognitive behavioural therapy (also referred to as CBT) is another evidence-based strategy that has been used for a long time and has proven helpful to a lot of people. While it is a behavioural approach like ACT, it's focus is slightly different. It focuses on the thought rather than accepting the thought and focusing on value-actioned behaviour like ACT.

To put it in as simple terms as I can, one of the easiest ways I find to think about CBT is the ABC-DE approach. Let's break that down a little:

A = the 'activating event' or trigger
B = the belief you have because of the activating event
C = the consequences of your belief
D = disputing the belief
E = empowerment.

In CBT, the theory is that when you are suffering psychologically, it is due to your belief (B) about the activating event (A) being unhelpful in some way. As a result of this unhelpful belief, you then experience certain unhelpful consequences (C). To be able to address this in a more helpful way using CBT, the aim is to dispute (D) the thought into something more realistic or helpful, which then leads to empowerment (E).

Let's look at an example.

You go into the lunchroom at work and Judy comments on your messy hair and how awful you look, adding in the pun of 'look what the cat dragged in' (A). You immediately feel humiliated and embarrassed and run out of the room crying and thinking to yourself you are unattractive and stupid for believing Judy and the other staff like you (B). All the memories of being teased at school about your wild hair come flooding back, you start to feel as though you're not good enough, and you become distraught (C).

As with the above problem-solving approaches, you could use one of those strategies, but this time it seems it's hit something deep-down that is really concerning you. If you choose to use CBT you would then go back to the belief (B) — that is, you are unattractive and stupid for believing Judy and the other staff like you. At this point you want to start disputing (D) this belief, as it certainly is not helpful and quite possibly may not be realistic either. To do this you can ask yourself the following questions:

1. Is this belief helpful? (in other words, does it help you to feel good?).

2. Is this belief realistic? (in other words, is it realistic to think that just because Judy made a joke about your hair you are unattractive and stupid?).
3. Where is the evidence for this belief? (in other words, prove to me that this belief is 100% accurate. Prove to me you are unattractive and stupid — show me the evidence because I do not believe it).

Now ask yourself what other belief or thought you could have instead (D). Could you tell yourself that actually, your hair was pretty wild this morning because you got it caught up in one of the animal cages when you were leaning in to change the blankets? Could you tell yourself that Judy was just trying to lighten the mood and had no idea it was a sensitive issue for you? Could you tell yourself that just because your hair was messy it doesn't mean you are unattractive and stupid?

Once you go through these steps and realise that this is just a thought (which may not necessarily be true, helpful, or realistic) and you can come up with other healthier beliefs to dispute it, you then become empowered (E). You are not letting your thoughts control how you feel anymore — and this can be empowering!

Eye Movement Desensitisation and Reprocessing (EMDR)

EMDR is an evidence-based intervention developed over thirty years ago, originally for post-traumatic stress disorder (PTSD). However, it has proven effective for a range of different psychological disorders and issues and is actually one of my favourite strategies. I have seen some incredible changes with my clients who have undergone EMDR, as well as heard some brilliant outcomes with the clients of my psychology colleagues who also use EMDR.

While it can sound quite technical, I'll try and explain it in as simple terms as possible. Essentially, EMDR is about desensitising you to memories you have had (and the subsequent memory network of thoughts, feelings, emotions, and the range of senses involved) to something traumatic or triggering. I have found most of the time this goes back to something in childhood, but not always. Then the aim is to reprocess the belief underlying that memory into something more positive. So, it looks something like this:

When you were five years old your mum asked you to tidy your toys away before dad got home. Mum was cooking dinner (which happened to be your favourite – lasagne!), and you were watching your favourite television show. You vividly remember the smell of the lasagne going through the house, and could see how delicious it looked as mum was just about to pull it out of the oven. Dad came in and tripped on one of your toys and yells at you 'move your stupid toys! How can you be so stupid to leave the toy in the middle of the room? Use your brain you idiot! Now look what you've done — I've probably broken my toe because of you! Why can't you be more like your siblings who keep their things perfectly tidy?!' Mum then yelled at you again and said, 'I told you to put them away — now look what you've done!'

Wow — can you imagine going through something like this and all the thoughts running through your head? You may have started to think you are an idiot, you are stupid, and you will never be as good as your siblings – not to mention that in future you need to be perfect so something like this never happens again. The thought or belief around this could be 'I'm not good enough'. If no one corrects you and says to you that it's not your fault or that you're not really an idiot, it can then reinforce the negative belief and does not allow that memory to be processed adaptively (which means it is maladaptive).

Now imagine over time whenever something happens and you are in situations where you are compared to others or make an unlikely mistake with something — your immediate thought (belief) will likely revert back to not feeling good enough. The more this happens and the more the negative belief is reinforced, the more it can start to feel like the truth — and so you believe it.

It is important to caution here though that EMDR should only be done with a qualified EMDR practitioner and should not be attempted otherwise. To do so could be harmful and leave you stuck deep into those negative thoughts and memories. It is also important to note that going through an EMDR session can feel like going through a black tunnel — however, you wouldn't usually stop in the middle of the tunnel in the pitch black. Rather you would keep going until you reached the end of the tunnel. Likewise, with EMDR you may feel and experience some deep feelings and emotions, but it is generally suggested you keep going as they tend to subside as you progress through the session. Some people may not have intense reactions, but others will. As my colleagues and I say, 'your brain knows what it needs to do to heal itself — you just need to get out of its way and let it do the work'.

With EMDR we would typically look at what is currently going on for you (for example — feeling angry about Judy's comments relating to your hair, and how you felt stupid), and then we'd look at the emotions and feelings around this. Then we would ask you to think back to when you can recall feeling like this in the past — as far back as you can remember. All of a sudden, the memory of dad yelling at you because you didn't put your toys away comes flooding back. Ahhh – now we've got to the core (real, underlying) issue and core belief that 'I'm not good enough'! While you keep noticing this memory, you focus your eyes on the therapist's two fingers (which they will hold up) while they are moving them side-to-side in a particular way (or perhaps it could be using butterfly taps or some other bilateral movement). The aim is that you get bilateral movement (usually the eyes moving bilaterally, but again, it could be by way of butterfly taps), while you recall that initial memory. This continues until the subjective units of distress (SUDS) reduces to a certain level (which the therapist monitors). Once this is reached the therapist then reprocesses the belief with a more positive belief (generally, it is the opposite of the negative belief). So, in this particular case, as you recall that initial memory, you start to reprocess it but this time using the positive belief 'I did the best I could' until that reaches a certain level of belief (validity of cognition — or VOC).

Some people feel exhausted after an EMDR session as the brain does a lot of work. Others feel exhilarated as they have released so much of the trauma and/or negativity. Every person is individual, and as such, their experiences will be individual. The brain may continue to process for around 24–48 hours after the EMDR session, so it's important to just notice any thoughts or feelings and observe them — rather than buying into them. Often the same memory can still have some triggering effects even after an EMDR session — this can sometimes happen if the wrong core belief was used, or if there were multiple core beliefs attached to the same memory.

I like to describe the process as like a cyst on an animal. Imagine your brain with a separate 'blob' next to it, filled with all those negative memories, thoughts, feelings, visuals, etc., which have never been processed adaptively (aka healthily). Just like with a cyst, if you just keep draining it (i.e., tip of the iceberg/band-aid solution), it could still continue to keep filling up if you don't get to the core of what is causing it (i.e. the underlying issue or core problem). If you cut the cyst out and get to the core issue, it may be unlikely to keep filling up again. This is like what we are doing with EMDR — we are taking that memory, opening it up so everything comes out, then reprocessing it in a healthy way — just like cutting out the cyst and getting to the root cause.

EMDR does not necessarily take the memory away so you can never recall it, but it does usually make the memory seem distant and/or take the emotion out of it, so you can recall the memory but not be negatively affected by it like you once were.

It's no secret that I was once one of the queasiest people you could ever meet when it came to anything gory or involving blood (hence not pursuing my dream of becoming a veterinarian). I had EMDR myself and can now watch a lot more gory or bloody things, and my tolerance has certainly improved a great deal compared to what I used to be able to (or not able to!) for decades prior. It has definitely helped me on a personal level, which is why I am such an advocate for it.

In Summary

- It is important to recognise what is within your control, and what isn't.
- Practice mindfulness regularly so it becomes an automatic process.
- Work on your values to identify the things that are most important to you.
- Thoughts become things, so make sure you are not 'buying into' and believing every thought that comes into your head.
- Remember — just because you are thinking it, it doesn't mean it is true!

Chapter 15

Relaxation

Relaxation is an important part of our health and well-being. We need to be able to relax to keep our stress and anxiety levels at a manageable level. There are many different forms of relaxation, and finding what makes you feel relaxed is essential. Relaxation isn't just about sitting quietly and doing nothing (although some people find this relaxing!). We like to think of relaxation as essentially what makes you feel relaxed and helps you get that wonderful feeling of 'calm'.

Some of my favourite recommendations for relaxation include:

- sitting quietly and deep breathing
- listening to music
- dancing
- gardening
- exercising (walking, jogging, surfing etc.)
- arts and crafts (including colouring-in!)
- sitting at the beach and watching the ocean (a personal favourite of mine)
- being in nature

- stroking a pet (another favourite of mine)
- engaging in hobbies
- socialising with friends
- journalling.

Two easy but often beneficial strategies I have previously recommended are deep breathing and progressive muscle relaxation. We'll take a quick recap of these now before I talk about polyvagal exercises.

Deep breathing

Deep breathing can be an excellent way of relaxing and keeping a sense of 'calm'. It can also be very effective in helping with symptoms of anxiety. Best of all, it is completely free to do, and you can basically do it anywhere and anytime!

There are a few different strategies used for deep breathing. I prefer the following:

1. Breathe in (inhale) through your nose to a count of 3 or 4 (one and two and three and four).
2. You can hold it there for a second if you wish, although this is not essential.
3. Then, gently breathe out (exhale) through your mouth to the same count (one and two and three and four).
4. When you inhale, make sure it comes from your stomach/diaphragm first, then all the way up the top of the lungs. This enables oxygen to circulate to the brain (assisting with effective functioning). If you breathe from your chest (those short-shallow breaths we tend to take when stressed or anxious),

you are hyperventilating, which doesn't allow oxygen to flow to the brain properly.

You may also like to try 'box breathing' as follows:

1. Breathe in through the nose for a count of 4 (one and two and three and four).
2. Hold the breath for a count of 4 (one and two and three and four).
3. Breathe out through the mouth for a count of 4 (one and two and three and four).
4. Hold the breath for a count of 4 (one and two and three and four).
5. Repeat for a couple of cycles and notice if you are starting to feel calmer.

Progressive muscle relaxation

Progressive muscle relaxation is the process of tensing and then relieving selected muscle groups in a controlled manner. Please be mindful, though, that you should seek professional advice from your medical practitioner if you have any injuries to any area of your body before attempting progressive muscle relaxation.

Again, there are different ways that these can be done. I prefer the following:

1. Lie down (preferable — although it can be done in a seated position) in a comfortable position. Clench/tighten your feet as much as possible and hold for a couple of seconds. Then slowly release the tension.
2. Clench/tighten your calf muscles and hold for a couple of seconds. Then slowly release the tension.

3. Clench/tighten your upper legs and hold for a couple of seconds. Then slowly release the tension.
4. Repeat these steps using other parts of your body — for example buttocks, stomach, chest, shoulders, hands, mouth, nose, eyes etc.
5. Tighten the whole body and hold for a few seconds. then release.

The process of clenching/tightening tightens the muscles but then relaxes the muscle when released. This can be an effective way of releasing built-up tension in the muscles and can also help you to notice when you are tense and how to release that tension.

Polyvagal exercises

You may be familiar with or heard about, the vagal nerve. It is the 10th cranial nerve and runs from the base of the skull right down into the gut (it is also responsible for the gut-brain axis you may recall I spoke about when talking about the food-mood connection).

Think of this nerve like a tall tree. All the branches connect to different parts of the body and anatomy. Now imagine that it is on fire and inflamed — bright red roaring through your body, and everything connected to it is also negatively affected. This is what it can be like when you are anxious — the autonomic nervous system is affected, and the sympathetic (i.e., fight/flight) nervous system is activated. The body thinks it is about to be attacked by a predator and is preparing to stay and fight or take flight for its survival. Many things are happening in the body at a physiological level to prepare it to fight or take flight. It can be hard to think straight because the body is diverting things to other parts of the body.

Now imagine pouring cold water down the tip of that tree all the way to the base, putting out that fire and inflammation. This is what it's like when the parasympathetic (i.e., rest/digest) nervous system is activated. In this state, we feel nice and calm, relaxed, and not like we do when we are in the fight/flight state.

When we use polyvagal exercises, it's like we are pouring cold water on the autonomic nervous system and cooling it right down. Let's take a quick look at this in a bit more detail.

These exercises are from Stanley Rosenberg's book 'Accessing the Healing Power of the Vagus Nerve' and are designed as self-help exercises for various indications. As with all the suggestions in this book, it is important to note that this suggestion is provided for general information purposes only. Before administering any suggestions, individuals should seek advice from their health care provider. Any application of this material is at the reader's discretion and their sole responsibility.

> Step 1: Weave the fingers of each hand together and place them behind your head. Lie on your back at first. Once familiar with the exercise, you can choose to stand or sit on a chair.
>
> Step 2: With your hands behind the back of your head, rest the weight of your head comfortably on your interwoven fingers.
>
> Step 3: Keep your head in place (do not turn your head) and, moving only your eyes, look to the right as far as you comfortably can.

Step 4: After a short period of time (up to 30 or 60 seconds), you should automatically yawn, sigh, or swallow (which is a sign your autonomic nervous system is relaxing).

Step 5: Bring your eyes back to looking straight ahead (i.e., to the ceiling if lying down, or straight ahead if sitting or standing).

Step 6: Leaving your hands in place, keep your head still and then move your eyes to the left.

Step 7: Hold your eyes there until you again notice a yawn, sigh, or swallow.

Once you have completed the exercise, take your hands away and slowly sit up or stand up.

If you feel dizzy when you stand or sit up, it could be due to you relaxing while lying down and your blood pressure dropping. This is a normal reaction and usually takes a few minutes for your blood pressure to adjust and pump more blood to your brain.

I have personally found this exercise to be very helpful. Even though I am a psychologist and have a range of strategies in my toolbox, it doesn't mean I don't get triggered or stressed! I have noticed myself calm right down after using this strategy.

As I have mentioned several times now, just as with other strategies, it is important to find a routine or exercise that works for you (but remember my golden rule — it needs to be safe, healthy, and legal!). You might not do it perfectly the first few times, but the important thing to remember is that you are trying — and I think that is a great place to start!

Chapter 16

Resilience

What do you think of when you think of resiliency? Most commonly, I find people answer this question with 'the ability to bounce back'. While it is true that it *can* be the ability to bounce back from adversity, resilience is gained not only by experiencing some unfortunate event or tragedy but also by our successes. Resilience is not the same as being tough-minded, although it can be closely related — it can be found in both the brashest and quietest people.

So, what does a resilient person look like? Some of the characteristics of a person with a resilient mindset include:

- feeling as though they have control of their life
- possessing empathy and acting empathically
- knowing how to strengthen their hardiness for stress
- learning from failure and success
- having solid decision-making and problem-solving skills.

When we look at resilience, we can also look at both positive and negative scripts. A positive script is when a behaviour that leads to positive outcomes is repeated. However, on the opposite end are self-defeating or counter-productive behaviours, which, if continually repeated, will result in a negative script developing. Such negative scripts are obstacles to the development of a resilient mindset.

When we can accept that our life is going to involve a mixed bag of experiences that will be both positive and negative, it places us in a much better position to be able to deal with the life events that will undoubtedly be thrown at us from time to time. Being able to accept the things we can and cannot change in our life can be one of the most important factors in understanding resilience. Essentially this means accepting and learning not to put our energy and focus into the things that are not working so well for us but instead being able to grow and work with the things that are right in our lives.

Being able to develop the virtue of patience by solving problems and breaking them down into smaller, more manageable pieces is key to building resilience. So too is the ability to cultivate a sense of self-compassion for yourself and the experiences you have encountered. This involves being kind and gentle with yourself and undertaking pleasant personal activities such as helping others, eating well, exercising, and meditating.

In summary, being resilient involves learning how to effectively cope with the ups and downs of life by practising the things which support that coping capacity. Remember to recognise and acknowledge your successes rather than getting caught up in what you perceive as failures. After all, worrying about failures and berating yourself over them won't change the reality that they have happened. Instead, put that energy and attention into the things within your control— your behaviour, right here, right now! And don't forget to reach out for support if you need to.

Tips for building resiliency

My top 10 tips for building resiliency are:

1. Rewrite the negative scripts you use in your head and change the words of life to something more positive.
2. Rather than taking a stressed-out path, choose one that is stress-hardy instead.
3. View life through the eyes of other people. How do other people see you? How do they view the world?
4. Practice effective assertive communication.
5. Accept others as well as yourself. Remember, most of us are doing our best with what we've got. None of us are perfect.
6. Display compassion and make genuine connections with people.
7. Deal effectively with your mistakes by seeing them as opportunities to learn from rather than failures.
8. Build masses of competence by dealing well with success. Focus on the things you have done well rather than the things you didn't do as well.
9. Develop self-control and self-discipline.
10. Maintain a resilient lifestyle by being with resilient people and focusing on the positives in your life, not the negatives.

Chapter 17

Spirituality

Don't worry. This isn't trying to convert you to following some religious order. Rather it's about exploring a very human and ordinary part of our psychological makeup. Spirituality can be found in all cultures throughout history into the present day. Research has shown that it provides many people with an inner strength in life as a coping strategy to move through difficult times. When feeling isolated, it can help a person reconnect with something greater than themselves and experience self-compassion.

Spirituality is a personal experience. The belief in something that is greater than ourselves can take many forms. In that way, spirituality is different from religion. A person can be spiritual without overtly practising behaviours that are accepted as belonging to organised religion. Religion has spirituality as its basis but adheres to a formalised set of beliefs, practices and rituals.

Spirituality then can mean different things to different people. Some people refer to their spirituality as a specific religious belief, but for others, their spirituality may reflect more about their cultural beliefs or a private view of life being more than just a random set of events. For some, a feeling of grace, inner calm or spectacular joy may be achieved through a connection with nature that they feel brings something extra to their existence.

Faith in one's endeavours might involve believing in a power from within themselves or from something universal yet unquantifiable. For others, their spirituality may involve belief in angels or higher consciousness, psychic ability, or forms of extrasensory perception. For some, even a love and devotion to science or atheism provides an element of self-satisfaction and reward that may well play a similar role in our psychological makeup as a spiritual connection.

The point is that people have a spiritual side. So, getting in touch with your own spirituality (whatever that may mean to you) and having that trust and faith in something bigger than yourself is important to one's self-view and mental wellbeing. Intuition, or a belief in something or someone greater or more powerful than yourself, whatever it is, can be a large component of our self-care. Being able to meditate (at whatever level you are comfortable with) or even just sitting mindfully and connecting with your inner self can be calming. In my own experience, I set an intention prior to a daily personal meditation that helps to keep me relaxed. In fact, my blood tests have shown a positive correlation between my cortisol levels and meditation since I started practising meditation on an almost daily basis. There are plenty of resources and courses available for those who want to pursue meditation or yoga so keep searching until you find something that is a good fit for you.

Chapter 17 Spirituality

I understand though that meditation may not be for you. You need to find something you are comfortable with or believe in and use that as part of your daily self-care regime. So, if you believe in god, perhaps it is praying or reading the bible that gives you comfort. If you have different cultural beliefs relating to another religion, regularly engaging in those rituals will also give you comfort. If it helps you to take good care of yourself and is not dangerous, illegal, or unhealthy, then so be it. I believe it is important to find what works for you and try to incorporate those activities into your daily life as best as is practical.

I encourage you to think about what spirituality means to you. Granted, some of you may have no interest in spirituality whatsoever (and that's okay) but look deeper into why. Could it be that beneath all this, the real reason is that it scares you, or you don't understand it, or you don't want to be labelled a 'weirdo' — or is it that you just haven't really given it much thought and don't know where to get started?

Chapter 18

Motivation

Understanding the cycle of motivation (and all the different stages we go through) is important to recognise as it can explain why we may feel differently as time progresses. The model of motivation goes something like this:

The honeymoon stage:

- The Hype — where you might feel completely motivated by something and want to spend every waking moment involved with it.
- The Plummet — where suddenly you start to question the reason you started all this and you quickly lose all motivation, questioning yourself over the hype that started it.
- The Lapse — where there may be a temporary lapse in your motivation which may leave you feeling like you're no longer interested enough, but wish you were.

The surge stage:

- The Slips and Surges — where you feel you are on a roller coaster as you struggle with low motivation, then regain a surge of interest only to lose it again.

Temptation & habit bundling

I think the idea of temptation bundling is quite clever! It involves combining (or 'bundling') something you *want* to do with something you *should* do. This can be very helpful if you are not feeling very motivated to do something, so you bundle two or more activities together. As an example — if you love listening to music but don't love going outside to exercise, combine your exercise while you are listening to music (but of course make sure it is safe to do so and if outdoors you can still hear what is going on around you). Or perhaps it could be listening to some tunes while you do housework, watching your favourite TV show while you do the ironing, or listening to a great podcast while you drive to work.

Similar to temptation bundling is the concept of habit bundling. This is where you pair a habit you already have with another habit you want to start to develop. For example, practicing gratitude while you are eating a meal, doing some stretches while you are watching television, or practicing positive affirmations while you are showering.

While we're on the topic of habits, it might be a good time to mention neuroplasticity. Neuroplasticity is the brain's amazing ability to form new neural pathways and synaptic connections regarding the new experiences we have, things we learn, or even how to heal the body after sickness or injury. It is essentially about the way our brain can bounce back and grow and find other ways to make connections if it encounters an obstacle. Think about walking the same path every single day over your carpet or lawn. Eventually the carpet or lawn will start to get worn down — it's a bit like our brain. It gets so used to doing the same thing all the time, that it's become the status-quo. But if we want to find a new way to do something, we have to first teach our brain how to do it — walking on a different patch of carpet or lawn instead of the trodden-down way. After a period of time (it has been suggested that it takes 21 days to form a new habit) the brain remembers the new neural pathway it has just formed, and this then becomes the new way of doing things (aka the new habit). This isn't to say you won't still go the old way from time-to-time, but you're more likely to go the new way as this is what you have now programmed your brain to do.

Paving new pathways can even help to keep your brain young as every time you learn something new, you form a new neural pathway — so the more you learn and the longer you learn, the more you are creating new pathways. Even doing something you've always done a little differently can help to increase neuroplasticity.

What's more, aerobic (cardio) activity has been shown in research to increase neuroplasticity. Brain-derived neurotrophic factor (BDNF) is a growth hormone which helps to create, grow, and reshape new neurons and form synapses and it is produced when we move our bodies in this way, particularly when we pick up the pace with higher intensity activity like high intensity interval training or going for a sprint.

Self-efficacy

Self-efficacy can be described as a person's ability to act in a particular way to achieve a particular result. High self-efficacy tends to lead to high motivation. To help build your self-efficacy you can try to reflect on your successes and/or things that have gone well and then reinforce them.

Doing this can help you to acknowledge your accomplishments and increase your confidence in yourself and your ability to keep going.

Chapter 19

Exploring Core Beliefs

Are your core beliefs holding you back? For so many people, they absolutely are. They believe everything their mind tells them without mindfully checking how realistic those thoughts are.

Negative beliefs vs positive beliefs

In my work as a psychologist, I see people's negative beliefs come into action virtually every day. Some of the most common ones I come across are 'I'm not good enough', 'I'm unlovable', 'I'm not perfect', and 'I should have done more'. Does any of this sound familiar?

Negative beliefs are generally unhelpful, unrealistic, and often not even true. In my experience, they usually don't help you to live a happy and content life full of wellbeing. A positive belief is usually more helpful (even though it still may not be true) but is generally helping you to feel more content with yourself and feel more of a sense of wellbeing.

Imagine the following two statements and think about which makes you feel better.

'I am stupid and not good enough — what was I thinking? I'm an idiot!'

versus

'I did the best I could with the knowledge and experience I had at the time.'

I know which one I prefer, and it's not the first one! Imagine if all the stories your mind told you were negative like this. It doesn't take long before the pessimism kicks in and takes over if you continually have a negative mindset and beliefs.

While I find traditional talk therapy can be beneficial for my clients, I like to use EMDR (see Chapter 14) to help them get to the core of the issue they are dealing with — that is, deep down, way below the surface level (or tip of the iceberg) stuff. If we don't get to the core issues, how can we expect to move forward in a psychologically healthy way if we just keep patching things up with band-aids?

Mindset & thought distortions

In a nutshell, your mindset can be described as the way you think about things — your assumptions, your beliefs, and how you process and make sense of things. There are two general types of mindsets — fixed and growth.

Fixed mindset

A person with a fixed mindset typically believes that talents are something people are born with, and unless you are born gifted or good at something, there is essentially nothing you can do to change that. They may also be fixed and rigid in their thought patterns and will not deviate from them — 'there is only one way to do this, and nothing else will work'.

Growth mindset
In contrast, a person with a growth mindset believes that we can improve ourselves and learn to develop the things we are good at with relatively little effort. They are generally more likely to be open to growth and development — 'while things have always been done this way in the past, there may be new things we could try that will help to improve this'.

So let's just take a quick look at some unhelpful thought patterns that can distort your ability to pursue a mindset that helps you deal with the stressors you come across.

Thought distortions (aka 'lies')
Have you ever looked at someone else and thought they have it all together and their life must be perfect because they have a nice car, great job, fantastic figure, or some other thought? It's easy to assume they have the best life imaginable, but how do you know? How do you know they're not struggling to pay their car loan, hate their job, and have just spent the last 12 months working incredibly hard to eat healthily and lose weight? It can be very misleading (and unhelpful!) to make assumptions about other people. Remember the saying 'the grass is always greener on the other side'? (Note to self: it's not always!)

This type of thinking can be a great example of thought distortions. Thought distortions may also be known as unhelpful thinking styles. They are ways our thoughts become distorted — or not always aligned with the truth or reality. One of the problems with distorted thinking is that we are often just seeing one part of the situation, but we do not necessarily see it in the context of the entire situation.

Shoulds, musts, and have-tos
When you tell yourself you should, must, or have to do something, you can set yourself up to fail. Try reframing this. First of all, start by asking yourself if you want to and need to. The rule of thumb here is if the answer is yes, then you should do it, but if the answer is no, then you shouldn't do it (but make sure it is not something unsafe, unhealthy, or illegal!). Instead of saying 'I should do...', replace this with 'I want to...' (assuming you want to). If you don't want to do it, then say, 'I can go to...instead' or 'if i choose'.

The inner critic
Ah, the inner critic! That little voice in your head that jumps to conclusions and tells you that you are not as good as everyone else, that you should be doing much better, or that you must act a certain way because people will like you more if you do. Your inner critic doesn't always have anything helpful to say — it compares oranges to apples rather than comparing apples with apples. That's because you are unique, and there is no one the same as you!

Decision fatigue
Generally, the quality of choices tends to decrease as the day progresses, so it may be helpful to take time earlier in the morning to make decisions about things that are happening rather than making them later in the day or evening.

Fallacies
Mistaken beliefs are known as fallacies and are normally based on unsound arguments. Rather than buying into these, it is better to focus on acceptance of the reality of what is, rather than unhelpful thoughts and distorted thinking.

What can you do about it?
If you are struggling with your thoughts, remember the recommended strategies from ACT. If things are still getting the better of you, a relatively quick-and-easy tip is to notice the thought and then ask yourself why it may not be accurate. Try to identify the distortion that your mind is generating. Once you have identified the distortion, you can acknowledge that this is not true or helpful, and then counter this. Ask yourself what *is* the truth, or what *would* be helpful. Thinking of your values and acting in line with them is one of the best ways to respond to these distortions.

Alternatively, you may also build up your tolerance by acknowledging the frustration but choosing to act appropriately. For example — 'even though I feel angry right now, I will just do some deep breathing to calm myself down rather than respond angrily'.

Don't forget — thoughts become things, and just because you are thinking it, it doesn't mean it's true! Thoughts are just words, stories our mind tells us, and whether we believe them or not is up to us. Ideally, choosing positive thoughts or affirmations is the preference as it has been shown these can directly affect your daily experiences, choices you make, your nervous system, your outlook on life, and your interactions with other people.

Speaking of affirmations, did you know they have been proven to assist in strengthening good habits, building confidence, building self-efficacy, reducing doubt and fear, and helping to break bad habits?

Chapter 20

Mental Health Problems need Mental Health Solutions

I am a firm believer that mental health problems need mental health solutions — from qualified mental health professionals. I see many unqualified people offering mental health and wellbeing support, and quite frankly, it scares and frustrates me!

It scares me because mental health is not a game. Just because we all deal with some level of mental health ourselves, it does not mean we are qualified to help others with theirs. It's like me saying that because I have been a pet owner for decades, I should be able to advise other pet owners on how they should care for their pets. Without being a qualified veterinary professional, I cannot possibly expect to know everything there is to know — and my unqualified advice could have detrimental and even life-threatening effects — ditto for mental health.

The frustration comes from how blasé some people seem to talk about such things as *mental health coaching* or *wellbeing coaching*. To set up shop as a 'coach' in this space without a recognised degree in the psychological sciences and the appropriate professional registration as a treatment provider makes a mockery of the many years of study qualified mental health professionals need to undertake. As a colleague of mine once sarcastically joked, 'how hard can it be, right?'.

It is crucial to understand that mental health has many layers, and it is not a one-size-fits-all scenario. Unless you were appropriately trained, how would you know that your coaching client is not experiencing suicidal thoughts beneath their outwardly positive demeanour? Would you know how to handle the situation if they told you out of the blue that they wanted to kill themselves? This situation has happened to one of my psychologist peers. Fortunately, she was trained to be able to deal with the situation appropriately — but I fear many unqualified people wouldn't be so well equipped.

But I also understand that there can be some confusion about all the different roles out there. So let's break that down a bit.

First, think about why you need to approach someone for help and how you feel and think about yourself and your current life experience. Would you go to your mechanic for a haircut? Would you undergo surgery with your local store assistant? Unless they were qualified in these areas, I would certainly hope the answer is no!

Many people, however, find there is a lot of stigma in seeing a qualified mental health professional such as a psychologist or psychiatrist. They would rather try and use 'band-aid' quick-fix solutions in the hope of a fast 'cure' — something that doesn't involve the effort, time and self-exposure of therapy. Perhaps they might find a book that tells them they need only think differently, and they will gain the power to improve quickly. I'm sorry to say to you, but there is generally no quick fix or magic pill to 'cure' people of their psychological disorders. Changing how one thinks and behaves to ease emotional distress takes work, support, and dedication, usually with the help of qualified mental health practitioners. I have had many clients come to me for the first time and tell me they have 'tried everything and nothing worked'. When I ask them what they have tried, it usually consists of a simplified solution offered by an unqualified practitioner. This can make the job of helping the person feel better that much harder, as I need to deal with resistance from the client as they believe nothing will help them and correct any psychological damage caused by the unqualified person claiming to 'cure' them.

Coaching, counselling, psychology, and psychiatry

With both regulated and unregulated mental health professionals working here in Australia and around the world, it is important to be informed about the different professionals and how they may be able to help you. It is essential to increase your knowledge about the mental health professionals out there so you can make the best decision for yourself. Remember, do your research. Your mental health is not something to be 'played' with — it is serious stuff and can literally be a matter of life and death. Let's try and make sure it's the former, please.

Life coaches
While 'life coaching' has been around for quite some time, the popularity of coaching has somewhat evolved with the

introduction of social media influencers and multi-level marketers.

Usually, coaches claim to provide individuals with ways to positively influence their lives by working with them through 'coaching' sessions or programs, often at relatively high or inflated prices compared to their lack of qualifications and experience. Inspirational quotes and advice unfortunately seem to be a fundamental underpinning of these self-appointed 'wellness experts'. It is important to note currently (at least in Australia anyway) that while coaching associations exist, there is no governing body to regulate the life coaching industry. Sadly, this can result in well-intentioned amateurs providing advice — regardless of whether this advice is good, bad, or even harmful.

There are, of course, coaches out there who do some good work in life aspects not explicitly related to psychological distress and I have worked with coaches myself. Still, I would caution against seeing anyone unqualified promoting themselves as a coach for mental health. Please be sure to do your research before you consider engaging a coach.

Counsellors

As with life coaching, there is also currently no regulatory body in Australia for counsellors. This means anyone can call themselves a counsellor, so again, I would encourage you to use caution and do your research to ensure the person you may be considering working with is registered with a professional body such as the Australian Register of Counsellors and Psychotherapists.

Counsellors are often engaged to assist people working through their personal and emotional issues, with this type of treatment typically being short-term as it focuses on resolving the singular issue the individual is struggling with. Typically counsellors encourage understanding and self-development to support people making positive life changes. This process relies on a strong interpersonal relationship between the individual and the counsellor. Counsellors use this relationship to provide knowledge and insight into the specific areas in which they are trained.

I would add here though, that just because a counsellor isn't always a psychologist (but many times is), it doesn't mean they aren't good at what they do — and likewise, just because someone is a qualified psychologist, it doesn't always make them a good counsellor. I have known some non-psychologist counsellors who have worked well with their clients. Again, if you are considering undergoing counselling, then please do your research first.

Psychologists
Here in Australia (and in many parts of the world), psychology is a regulated profession that requires a minimum of six years of training to practice as a registered psychologist. This training includes a minimum of four years tertiary study and two years of supervised clinical practice (known as the 4 + 2 pathway). At the time of writing, however, some changes are coming into practice that will require a minimum of five years tertiary study followed by one year of supervised clinical practice (known as the 5 + 1 pathway). Psychologists are not required to be medical doctors first, nor can they prescribe medication.

Psychologists can provide counselling with a greater knowledge of the scope of mental health issues, including mood disorders, personality disorders, and intellectual disorders. Psychology itself is a science which is why these trained professionals offer a deeper understanding of mental health concerns. Additionally, training as a psychologist requires a research focus which generally means your psychologist uses evidence-based therapies in treatment.

The work of psychologists can be incredibly varied, from providing assessment and therapy, conducting psychological research, facilitating organisational or social change, and administering psychological tests. The scope of psychological work spans several industries, highlighting these professionals' importance. Psychologists may work in settings such as organisational, educational, health, forensic, with children, neuropsychological, and clinical.

Please note though, that you don't need to be experiencing a diagnosed mental disorder to see a psychologist — they can help with various life issues and concerns. Sports psychologists, in particular, work to improve performance and enhance resilience in competition.

Psychiatrists
Psychiatrists are medical doctors who continue their studies and specialise in mental health. They must undertake tertiary studies to become a medical doctor, followed by further training to specialise in psychiatry, and this can take approximately 11 years of formal training.

Like psychologists, a psychiatrist can offer a range of therapies for individuals struggling with mental health

Chapter 20 Mental Health Problems need Mental Health Solutions

issues, as well as having the ability to prescribe psychological medications. As such, they often treat people with more severe mental illnesses that require medication. Both psychologists and psychiatrists are trained to understand how the brain thinks and behaves using therapies such as counselling or psychotherapy to address any issues.

Chapter 21

Mentally Healthy Workplaces

Not all our stress comes from our personal life — in fact, a lot of stress comes from our work. Given many people spend such a large proportion of time in the workplace, ideally, you want this to be a source of enjoyment and gratification and not somewhere that makes you feel sick at the thought of being there.

I actually studied workplace conflict for my fourth-year psychology thesis and whether there was a correlation between conflict in the workplace and one's intention to leave the organisation. My hypotheses were supported — meaning that if there is unresolved conflict in the workplace, those involved are more likely to leave as a result. This can obviously have catastrophic implications for the organisation, particularly when it comes to productivity, absenteeism, commitment, job satisfaction, stress, and intention to leave — which can all affect the organisation's bottom line.

Let's look at what a mentally healthy workplace is and some of the things you could do to try and make yours a great place to work.

What is a mentally healthy workplace?

A mentally healthy workplace has many different attributes, some of which include the following:

- open and honest leadership
- mental health support
- prioritising mental health education
- managing workloads
- consideration of a work/life balance
- developing employee's skills and knowledge
- cultivating a respectful, fair, and trusting culture
- allowing employee influence and inclusion
- implementing good job design and working arrangements.

Implications of a mentally unhealthy workplace

There are some warning signs to be aware of that could indicate there are potential issues in the workplace. These may include the following.

- Behavioural signs. For example, staff being late to work and/or their behaviour is out of character.
- Emotional signs. For example, staff may appear angry, irritable, and/or sensitive, which is uncharacteristic of them.
- Physical signs. For example, staff may experience illnesses, weight issues, or other health problems in the absence of a pre-existing medical condition.
- Cognitive signs. For example, staff may have a lack of concentration, make mistakes, or may not be paying attention.

- Workplace conflict. Indications of this include high turnover, absenteeism, and/or loss of productivity.

Workplace conflict

As I mentioned, some people spend a large proportion of their lives at work, and many get to enjoy this process without having to deal with conflict at the same time. However, others are not so fortunate; sometimes, through no fault of their own, they can experience conflict with others at work.

Conflict's impacts on the organisation and individual can be very serious. From my research, I found that regardless of whether a worker is full-time or part-time, conflict is related to productivity, stress, job satisfaction, commitment, and intention to leave the organisation. Job satisfaction was also shown to have a negative impact on absenteeism — meaning that if a worker is dissatisfied with their job, they are more likely to be absent.

Workplace conflict should be taken seriously. Regardless of whether the conflict is with a co-worker or supervisor, it can negatively affect the bottom line of the business in these areas, as I have already stated:

- productivity
- absenteeism
- job satisfaction
- commitment
- stress
- intention to leave.

High turnover

If you have high turnover in your workplace, this could indicate you have a mentally unhealthy workplace and could relate to your staff experiencing (amongst other things):

- exhaustion
- lack of job satisfaction
- lack of career opportunities
- poor or negative working conditions
- workplace conflict
- low commitment, low job satisfaction (= higher intention to leave).

Other implications

There are also links between low interpersonal communication, boredom, and unsatisfactory relationships between management and employees. Incompetent supervisors who do not communicate relevant information to staff are a significant source of stress. Stress can then result in:

- low morale
- low motivation
- depression
- burnout
- absenteeism
- increase in turnover.

Some of the signs of stress within individuals can include:

- fatigue
- headaches

- coronary problems
- paranoia
- irritability
- depression
- anxiety.

Some steps you can take

Organisations can take a proactive approach to developing a mentally healthy workplace, and this is an area of my own work I really enjoy working with corporate clients on. Seeing the benefits of a mentally healthy workplace can be very rewarding! Some of the proactive steps organisations can take include:

- Suicide prevention. This involves reducing the stigma, encouraging people to speak up about how they are feeling, and having appropriate suicide prevention measures in place.
- Combatting stigma. Would you think twice about going to a doctor if you hurt your hand? If not, why think twice if you have something going on in your brain?
- Improving mental health literacy. This is about making it okay to speak up, and educating staff on mental health issues.
- Adopting a culture of anti-bullying. This means zero tolerance, with no excuse for abuse, no matter how stressed someone feels.
- Addressing work practice risk. This can include clear communication in the workplace about

working hours, shift work and job roles, all of which can be significant contributors to stress levels.
- Supporting employees experiencing mental health issues. This can include employee assistance programs or other support services and resources.
- Promoting a culture of wellbeing and positive mental health This might include having wellbeing programs that your staff can contribute to, such as team building days or self-care days.

The ideal mentally healthy workplace

Ideally, a mentally healthy workplace is one with excellent communication — that is, honest, open, and transparent communication. It is also integral to have great leaders and managers who lead the way (transformational leadership rather than transactional leadership) and model excellent behaviour while also being capable and supportive. Mentally healthy workplaces should also promote self-care, psychological health and safety, and provide flexible practices and psychological safety while ensuring the workplace culture is dignified and respectful.

Mentally healthy workplaces should also include the following:
- the provision of appropriate, easy-to-access, adequate support and resources for all staff
- listening to employees and taking their concerns seriously
- building a culture of trust
- peer support mentoring/buddy programs
- regular debriefing and checking in with staff

- listening, remaining non-judgemental, and being reassuring.

In summary

The implications of a mentally unhealthy workplace can have disastrous and serious consequences. We all have a right to work in a healthy and safe environment — this sometimes means speaking up if something is not right and not putting up with things that are unhealthy.

You have a voice — don't be afraid to use it assertively for positive change.

Chapter 22

The Importance of Hope and Optimism

I've saved the best until last! Hope and optimism for positive mental health are some of my absolute favourite things. Did you know that my name even means 'hope', so it seems I've always been destined for it!

When you think of positive mental health, what do you think of? It may surprise you to know that positive mental health is not just the absence of mental illness; rather, it can be described as a 'presence'. So that means a 'presence' of positive mental health.

If we take a quick look at positive psychology and the five pillars of wellbeing (PERMA) (I wrote more about these in my earlier book *Coping with Stress and Burnout as a Veterinarian*), we can apply these to positive mental health. PERMA stands for:

- the presence of positive emotion
- the presence of engagement
- the presence of meaning

- the presence of good relationships
- the presence of accomplishment.

In other words — the presence of flourishing.

Positive psychology

Typically, medicine and psychology have focused on pathology. However, positive psychology turns that on its head by focusing instead on the strengthening effects of events that are benevolent. Its research basis follows four main approaches:

- learned helplessness studies
- studies involving mastery (things that are escapable)
- studies involving helplessness (things that are inescapable)
- studies involving control (no effects).

Helplessness
It is interesting to note that studies have shown that, at least in a laboratory setting, people do not readily become helpless when they believe their setbacks in life are local, temporary, and changeable. That would indicate that they learn how to become helpless — that is, learned helplessness. Dr Martin Seligman (credited with being the founder of positive psychology) even researched how you can 'unlearn' helplessness which is very encouraging.

Optimism
This study is a favourite of mine, especially as it is linked to optimism. The study went something like this. In the mid-1980s, 120 men from San Francisco who had their first heart attacks served in an untreated control

group in a large study. They were all interviewed about their jobs, hobbies, and family. There was also a lot of information about their heart attacks, which was stored in a sealed envelope.

So, what happened? Within eight-and-a-half years, 50% of these men had died from their second heart attack. The researchers then opened the sealed envelope — what do you think the risk factors identified? Despite medical issues, only pessimism predicted a second heart attack! Out of the 16 most pessimistic men, only one didn't die from a second heart attack. Of the 16 most optimistic men, there were only five who died.

Happy people commonly do not complain much — reporting better general health and less pain and illness symptoms. Sad people, in contrast, report worse health and tend to have more complaints about pain.

In another study, this time led by Sheldon Cohen, Professor of Psychology at Carnegie Mellon University, it was found that people with high positive emotion before being injected with rhinovirus developed fewer colds than those whose positive emotion was average. Subsequently, those with average positive emotion were found to get fewer colds and flu than those with low positive emotions. But why is this so? In this study, they found the main difference was an inflammation-causing protein called interleukin-6. The lower the interleukin-6, the higher the positive emotion — hence less inflammation.

There are some theories about why optimists are less vulnerable to disease, such as:

- more social support through contact with friends and loved ones in your life relates to less illness

- sociable people are generally healthier than those who are lonely
- social networks are less rich in unhappy people than they are in happy people
- biological considerations are believed to play a role in those identified as optimists:
    - blood from optimists has been shown to produce more white blood cells (infection-fighting) than those who were pessimists
    - the genes of optimistic and happy people may well ward off cancer or cardiovascular disease
- the optimist is generally able to cope better with stress
- optimists tend to have healthier lifestyles and take action (while pessimists tend to believe they are helpless and nothing can be done to help things, optimists believe their actions do matter)
- optimists usually act on medical advice and take better care of themselves
- happy people were also found to sleep better than those who were unhappy, have high satisfaction with life (generally having a high relation with optimism) and are more likely to exercise more frequently, eat healthy diets, and not smoke.

Learning optimism

The great news is that you can learn how to become more optimistic. Dr Martin Seligman has even written a book on it! If you're interested, the book is called, not surprisingly, *Learned Optimism*.

While the strategies in Seligman's book tend to focus on CBT (which may help you to become more optimistic), I also believe the strategies from other modalities, such as ACT, can be helpful.

Firstly, I recommend you take the Values in Action (VIA) survey to identify where hope and optimism rank within your 24 character strengths. You can take this survey for free by visiting the following link and completing the questionnaire.

http://positivepsychsolutions.pro.viasurvey.org

If the character strength of hope and optimism is already in your top five character strengths, there's a pretty good chance you are quite optimistic already. If it is lower down on the list (particularly towards your lower 20–24 strengths) then you need to pay attention!

As a 'realistic' optimist myself, I'm going to share with you a few of my favourite tips — so hang tight!

When faced with a negative situation and your thoughts automatically go on autopilot to doom and gloom and expecting the worst, stop and ask yourself:

- are these thoughts realistic?
- is there any evidence to support or prove this thought or belief is correct?
- are these thoughts helpful?

I then suggest using strategies from ACT to determine how best to respond in line with your values.

Instead of assuming the worst-case scenario, instead, try asking yourself:

- what's the *best* outcome I could expect (rather than the worst)?

- what *do* I want (rather than what don't I want)?
- what if it *doesn't* happen (instead of getting consumed with what you think will happen)?

It can also be helpful to focus on gratitude and the things you *do* have rather than what you *don't* have:

- keep a gratitude diary or list and complete 10 things you are grateful for every day — there is always something
- focus on the good things about you/others/your circumstances rather than the bad or not-so-good things
- look for the best in people, not the worst.

In Summary

Even though your mind is probably telling you that you can't be optimistic, you don't have to believe it or act as if it were true!

Thoughts are just words. They are not always true.

Here's to your Wellbeing

I hope you have enjoyed this book as much as I've enjoyed writing it. I also hope you take this seriously and take an honest look at your self-care practices — are they helping you to love the life you live? Are you feeling great with a sense of contentment and wellbeing most of the time? If not, you can do something proactive about it — take control of your life and seek professional support if necessary.

There is no shame in doing so — in fact, I believe it is a sign of strength to reach out and admit you can't do everything on your own (realistically, how many of us can?).

I started formally studying psychology way back in 1996. My interests over the years have changed and grown, but I have always focused on a positive and optimistic mindset and being in the best health I possibly can. Have I been able to do this all on my own? No, of course not! I have reached out to expert integrative medical doctors, functional nutritionists, exercise scientists and physiologists, physiotherapists, business and marketing coaches, friends, colleagues, and a few others along the way to help me on my own health and wellbeing journey.

I have experienced setbacks and challenges like others, but I always try to take an optimistic approach and expect the best.

I feel incredibly fortunate that I have a background and expertise in psychology, and it has served me well over the decades where I have been able to make sure I am taking just as good care of myself as I do my loved ones and clients.

I encourage you to put yourself first and take a deep dive into the areas of your life that need a positive overhaul. Then set some SMART goals and start implementing your self-care routine as soon as possible! The sooner you get started, the sooner you can hope to see positive results.

Thank you for sharing this journey with me. I wish you all the very best for your self-care and wellbeing, and I hope that you, too, will live a life worth living!

Bibliography

Anonymous. (n.d.-b). *Compassion Fatigue Awareness Project.* Retrieved from http://www.compassionfatigue.org/

Australian Counselling Association. (2021). https://www.theaca.net.au/

Australian Psychological Society. (2021). *What is a psychologist?* https://www.psychology.org.au/for-the-public/about-psychology/what-is-a-psychologist

Beer, C. (2015). *Healthy Habits: 52 ways to better health.* Summer Hill, NSW, Australia: Rockpool Publishing

Beer, C. (2020). *Your Best Year Ahead: Small, easy steps to wellness.* Summer Hill, NSW, Australia: Rockpool Publishing

Brooks, R., & Goldstein, S. (2004). *The Power of Resilience.* United States of America: McGraw-Hill.

Centre for Clinical Interventions. (2021). *Self Esteem.* Retrieved from https://www.cci.health.wa.gov.au/Resources/For-Clinicians/Self-Esteem

Gable, S. L., & Haidt, J. (2005). What (and Why) is Positive Psychology? *Review of General Psychology, 9*(2), 103-110. doi:10.1037/1089-2680.9.2.103

Hamilton, N. (2019). *Coping with Stress and Burnout as a Veterinarian.* Samford Valley, Qld Australia: Australian Academic Press

Harris, R. (2009). *ACT Made Simple - A quick start guide to ACT basics and beyond.* Oakland, CA: New Harbinger Publications, Inc.

Hayes, S. C. (2004). Acceptance and Commitment Therapy, Relational Frame Theory, and the Third Wave of Behavioral and Cognitive Therapies. *Behavior Therapy, 35,* 639-665.

Hayes, S. C., Barnes-Holmes, D., & Roche, B. (2001). *Relational Frame Theory: A Precis.* Kluwer Academic Publishers, 160.

Hayes, S. C., Luoma, J. B., Bond, F. W., Masuda, A., & Lillis, J. (2006). Acceptance and Commitment Therapy: Model, processes and outcomes. *Behavior Research and Therapy, 44*, 1-25.

Hoare, P., McIlveen, P., & Hamilton, N. (2012). Acceptance and commitment therapy (ACT) as a career counselling strategy. *International Journal for Educational and Vocational Guidance, 12*(3), 171-187. doi:10.1007/s10775-012-9224-9

Hyman, M. (2019). *The Broken Brain Series*. Retrieved from https://drhyman.com/brokenbrain/

Johnstone, M. (2015). *The Big Little Book of Resilience*. New South Wales, Australia: Pan Macmillan Australia Pty Ltd.

Kubler-Ross, E. (1997). *The Wheel of Life: A memoir of living and dying*. New York, NY: Scribner Publishing

Lees, J. (2014). *Secrets of Resilient People*. Great Britain: Hodder and Stoughton.

Linley, P. A., Joseph, S., & Boniwell, I. (2003). Positive Psychology - Fundamental Assumptions. *The Psychologist, 16*(3), 126-143.

Longo, P. (2019). *The Gifts Beneath Your Anxiety: Simple Spiritual Tools to Find Peace, Awaken the Power Within and Heal Your Life*. United States of America: Citadel Press

MacErlean, B. (2013). [Personal communication]

Martin, D. (2021). Food Mood & Menopause. [Personal communication]

Miller, A. (2008). A Critique of Positive Psychology — or 'The New Science of Happiness'. *Journal of Philosophy of Education, 42*(3-4), 591-608.

National Mental Health Commission. (2021). *Mentally Healthy Workplaces*. Retrieved from https://www.mentalhealthcommission.gov.au/projects/mentally-healthy-work/national-workplace-initiative

Noom. (2021). *Stop dieting. Get Results*. Retrieved from https://www.noom.com

Peterson, C. (2006). *A Primer in Positive Psychology*. New York: Oxford University Press, Inc.

Peterson, C., & Seligman, M. (2004). *Character Strengths and Virtues. A handbook and classification*: Oxford University Press and American Psychological Association.

Peterson, C., & Seligman, M. (2005). *VIA Inventory of Strengths.* from Values in Action Institute

Positive Psychology.Com (2018). *How to set healthy boundaries and build positive relationships.* Retrieved from https://positivepsychology.com/great-self-care-setting-healthy-boundaries/

Ramsay, D. (2021). Nutritional Psychiatry for Healthcare Practitioners. [Personal communication]

Rosenberg, S. (2017). *Accessing the Healing Power of the Vagus Nerve: Self-help exercises for anxiety, depression, trauma, and autism.* Berkeley, California: North Atlantic Books

Royal Australian and New Zealand College of Psychiatrists. (2013). *The role of the psychiatrist in Australia and New Zealand* https://www.ranzcp.org/newspolicy/policy-and-advocacy/position-statements/role-of-psychiatrist-in-australia-and-new-zealand

Seligman, M. (2002). *Authentic Happiness.* Milsons Point, NSW Australia: Random House Australia Pty Ltd.

Seligman, M. (2011). *Flourish: A visionary new understanding of happiness and well-being.* New York, USA: Free Press.

Seligman, M. (1968). *Learned Optimism.* Milsons Point, NSW Australia: Random House Australia Pty Ltd

Seligman, M., & Csikszentmihalyi, M. (2000). Positive Psychology — An Introduction. *American Psychologist*, 55(1), 5-14.

Seligman, M., Ernst, R. M., Gillham, J., Reivich, K., & Linkins, M. (2009). Positive Education: positive psychology and classroom interventions. *Oxford Review of Education*, 35(3), 293-311.

Seligman, M., Steen, T., Park, N., & Peterson, C. (2005). Positive Psychology Progress - Empirical Validation of Interventions. *American Psychologist*, 60(5), 410-421.

Starkey, A. (2021). Sleep and nutrition. [Personal communication]

Stebbins, P. (2008). *Turning Stress into Success: You Can Cope! Work/life balance, stress, anxiety & depression*. Paddington, Qld, Australia: PsyHealth Media

Steinberg, S. B. (2007). *Positive psychology and schooling: An examination of optimism, hope, and academic achievement*. (Doctor of Philosophy in Education Dissertation), University of California, Berkeley, United States. (UMI 3275612)

Taylor, G. (2020). Eye Movement Desensitisation and Reprocessing. [Personal communication]

Tucker, R. P., Wingate, L. R., O'Keefe, V. M., Mills, A. C., Rasmussen, K., Davidson, C. L., & Grant, D. M. (2013). Rumination and suicidal ideation: The moderating roles of hope and optimism. *Suicide Research: Selected Readings*. Volume 10 - May 2013-October 2013.

Vey Voda-Hamilton, D. (2015). *Nipped in the Bud, Not in the Butt: How to Use Mediation to Resolve Conflicts over Animals*. United States of America: CreateSpace Independent Publishing Publishing Platform

Wrzesniewski, A. (n.d.). *Work-life questionnaire*. Retrieved from www.authentichappiness.org

Wrzesniewski, A., McCauley, C., Rozin, P., & Schwartz, B. (1997). Jobs, Careers, and Callings: People's Relations to Their Work. *Journal of Research in Personality*, 31(1), 21-33. doi:http://dx.doi.org/10.1006/jrpe.1997.2162

Yale University. (2021). Resilience. Retrieved from https://medicine.yale.edu/news/yale-medicine-magazine/article/resilience/

www.ingramcontent.com/pod-product-compliance
Lightning Source LLC
Chambersburg PA
CBHW061308110426
42742CB00012BA/2097